CONTENTS

Travel Guide

LONDON

NICK HANNA
UPDATED BY CAROL SYKES

NEW
HOLLAND

★★★ Highly recommended
★★ Recommended
★ See if you can

Sixth edition published in 2007
by New Holland Publishers (UK) Ltd
London • Cape Town • Sydney • Auckland
First published in 1997
10 9 8 7 6 5 4 3 2 1

website: www.newhollandpublishers.com

Garfield House, 86 Edgware Road, London W2 2EA
United Kingdom

80 McKenzie Street, Cape Town 8001
South Africa

14 Aquatic Drive, Frenchs Forest NSW 2086
Australia

218 Lake Road, Northcote, Auckland
New Zealand

ISBN 978 1 84537 657 4

Keep us Current
Information in travel guides is apt to change, which is
why we regularly update our guides. We'd be grateful
to receive feedback if you've noted something we
should include in our updates. If you have new
information, please share it with us by writing to the
Publishing Manager, Globetrotter, at the office nearest
to you (addresses on this page). The most significant
contribution to each new edition will receive a free
copy of the updated guide.

Although every effort has been made to ensure that this
guide is up to date and current at time of going to print,
the Publisher accepts no responsibility or liability for
any loss, injury or inconvenience incurred by readers
or travellers using this guide.

Publishing Manager: Thea Grobbelaar
DTP Cartographic Manager: Genené Hart
Editors: Nicky Steenkamp, Melany McCallum,
Thea Grobbelaar, Nic Orfang, Catherine Mallinick,
Gill Gordon, Rowena Curtis
Cartographers: Reneé Spocter, Nicole Bannister,
William Smuts, Éloïse Moss
Design and DTP: Lellyn Creamer, John Loubser
Compiler/Verifier: Elaine Fick
Reproduction by Hirt & Carter (Pty) Ltd, Cape Town. Printed
and bound by Times Offset (M) Sdn. Bhd., Malaysia.

Photographic Credits:
Action Plus/N. Tingle: p. 21; *Compliments of* **All England
Tennis and Croquet Club, Wimbledon:** p. 22; *Compliments
of* **Asprey & Garrard:** p. 49 (bottom); **Mark Azavedo Photo
Library:** pp. 15, 46, 103; *Compliments of* **The British
Museum:** p. 53; **Galerie Du Dragon,** *Compliments of* **Dalí
Universe:** p. 24; **A. Duncan:** pp. 65 (bottom), 107 (bottom);
P. Duncan: p. 36; **Gallo Images:** p. 40; *Compliments of* **The
Gilbert Collection:** p. 56; **Stephen Hansford:** p. 23;
Compliments of **Hard Rock Café:** p. 49; *Compliments
of* **Harrods:** p. 63; *Compliments of* **The Imperial War
Museum:** p. 14; **LF/A. Jumper:** p. 65 (top); **LF/B. Mayes:** p.
37; **LF/F. Torrance:** pp. 68, 111; **LF/A. Ward:** pp. 8, 20, 35,
39, 43, 87, 108, 109, 110; **O. Lim:** pp. 13, 27, 33 (bottom),
34 (top), 45 (top & bottom), 54, 55, 58, 62 (top & bottom),
66, 72, 82 (bottom), 90, 97, 106; *Compliments of* **Madame
Tussaud's London:** p. 82 (top & bottom); **Eric Nathan:** pp.
42, 96, 99, 102; **Photo Access:** p. 44; **Pictures Colour
Library:** cover, title page, pp. 17 (top), 66; **RHPL:** pp. 12,
16, 25, 50, 70, 76 (top); 86, 88, 89; **RHPL/C. Bowman:**
pp. 18, 77, 101; **RHPL/N. Boyd:** p. 107 (top); **RHPL/P.
Craven:** pp. 33 (top), 76 (bottom); **RHPL/ N. Francis:** pp. 4,
38 (bottom); **RHPL/P. Grundy:** p. 73; **RHPL/M. Jenner:** p.
57; **RHPL/ A.R. Lampshire:** p. 104; **RHPL/R. Rainford:** pp.
34 (bottom), 38 (top), 67, 74, 79, 94, 114; **RHPL/W.
Rawlings:** pp. 10, 75, 85, 95; **RHPL/ R. Richardson:** p. 30;
RHPL/E. Rooney: pp. 61, 64; **RHPL/N. Wood:** p. 17 (top);
RHPL/A. Woolfitt: pp. 11, 17 (bottom), 19, 26, 28, 29, 47,
92, 113; **P. Ryan:** p. 91; **Neil Setchfield:** pp. 38, 48; **Travel
Ink/I. Booth:** p. 112; **Travel Ink/M. Gargill:** p. 69; **Travel
Ink/P. Kingsford:** p. 7; **A. Williams:** p. 9; **P. Wilson:** pp. 6,
80, 83.
[LF: Life File; RHPL: Robert Harding Picture Library]

Cover: *The Millennium Bridge is a 330m (1083ft) steel
bridge linking South Bank with the City of London at
St Paul's Cathedral.*
Title Page: *A sundial in front of the Tower Bridge in the
city of London.*

1
Introducing London

'When a man is tired of London he is tired of life', wrote Samuel Johnson – a sentiment which is no less true today than it was in the 18th century. It is one of the great capitals of the world, the largest city in Europe, and the central focus of politics, the arts, entertainment, the media, the judiciary and much else in Britain itself.

For the visitor, London offers an endless pageant of history and tradition combined with the excitement of the avant-garde, a dizzying variety of entertainment, innumerable sporting events, a surprising number of parks and green spaces, culinary offerings that encompass almost every cuisine under the sun, and, of course, a vast selection of shops.

The well-known highlights – such as the Tower of London, Buckingham Palace, St Paul's Cathedral and other major monuments – attract scores of tour buses, but London also has many hidden corners which repay exploration, characterful backstreets which evoke the London of Charles Dickens, wonderful riverside or canal walks, unusual speciality museums, and tranquil Georgian squares.

Like any big city, London has its problems – crime, pollution, litter, spiralling property costs which are forcing key workers out of the capital – and the weather may not be the best in the world, but it still manages to extend a warm welcome to its 30 million or so annual visitors. London is a place which everyone has to visit at least once in their lifetime – it is one of the most dynamic, vibrant and exciting cities in the world.

TOP ATTRACTIONS

*** British Museum: the city's most popular attraction.
***London Eye: spectacular bird's-eye view of London
*** The National Gallery: one of the world's most important art collections.
*** Tower of London: living history in this medieval fortress.
*** St Paul's Cathedral: an enduring symbol in the heart of the city.
*** South Kensington museums: the city's finest.
*** Westminster Abbey: resting place of the monarchs.
**Madame Tussaud's: waxworks extravaganza.

Opposite: *A royal carriage leaving Buckingham Palace.*

Above: *Running through the heart of London, the River Thames has always played a crucial role in the city's history.*

THE LAND

In geological terms, most of the southeast of England is relatively young and dates back to between 135 and 70 million years ago. London itself lies mostly over sand and clay (in the north) and chalk and flint (in the south). Its defining geographical feature is the **River Thames**, which bisects the city and flows out via the Thames Estuary to the North Sea.

The Thames

In prehistoric times the 16km (10 mile) wide **Thames Valley** offered fertile soils, extensive woodlands and a plentiful water supply to the early settlers. The core of the city, dating back to Roman times, developed at the point nearest the mouth of the Thames, where it was both feasible to build bridges and to anchor large ships in deep water. The Thames is a **tidal** river, and extensive areas on either side of its banks are classified as flood plains. In Roman times, areas to the south of the river (such as today's Lambeth and Southwark) were swampy marshes and frequently inundated. Over the centuries the south-east of England has been gradually tilting towards the sea, and central London would still be subject to flooding from surge tides were it not for the **Thames Barrier** (*see* p. 103).

London was the first capital in the world to experience the Industrial Revolution, and the banks of the Thames are crammed with vestiges of the city's heyday as the centre of the British Empire.

Climate

London has a temperate climate, with the prevailing southwesterlies creating predominantly damp conditions. It's almost impossible to generalize about the weather in London, since it is highly changeable (perhaps this is why the weather always seems to feature so prominently in locals' conversations). Global climatic changes also seem

THAMES TRIPS

Although the Thames's role is not as pivotal as it once was, exploring the riverside history of London is nevertheless a great pleasure. The main wharves for the departure of river cruises are located at the Tower of London, Embankment (Charing Cross), Westminster, Waterloo (London Eye) and Greenwich. Several companies run regular services downriver to Greenwich all year and on to the Thames Barrier in summer. There are also extended sailings upriver to Kew, Richmond and Hampton Court. Travelcards and some Oyster cards provide discounts on many services. Details are obtainable from boat operators (*see* p. 121) and free booklets detailing boat services are available from tourist/travel information centres.

LONDON	J	F	M	A	M	J	J	A	S	O	N	D
AVERAGE TEMP. °F	41	41	45	49	55	61	65	64	59	53	46	43
AVERAGE TEMP. °C	5	5	7	9	13	16	18	18	15	12	8	6
HOURS OF SUN DAILY	1.5	2.4	3.3	4.9	6.0	6.0	6.1	6.3	4.6	3.5	2.0	1.3
RAINFALL ins.	2.0	1.3	1.7	1.8	1.9	2.1	1.5	1.9	2.2	2.4	2.1	2.1
RAINFALL mm	52	34	42	45	47	53	38	47	57	62	52	54
DAYS OF RAINFALL	11	8	10	9	9	8	7	7	9	9	9	10

to be having an impact, with unseasonal winter storms on the one hand and near-drought over the summer months on the other contributing to the unpredictability of weather forecasting. **Spring** (March, April, May) is generally a pleasant time to visit, although cold March winds and April showers can dampen the days; **summer** (June, July, August) often sees sweltering hot days (or weeks) followed by thunderstorms and overcast skies; **autumn** (September, October, November) can vary from hot, summer-like days in September to crisp, clear weather in October, with November traditionally one of the wettest months; **winter** (December, January, February) is a season you should come well prepared for, with cold conditions and rain, hail, sleet or even snow a possibility.

Plant Life

London's parks, squares and public gardens are home to a huge variety of plant life. In the Royal Parks stately oaks and other trees date back hundreds of years. **St James's Park**, east of Buckingham Palace, is one such, with a pleasing mix of hawthorn, plane and lime trees and weeping willows along the lake. **Regent's Park**, by contrast, is known for its displays of colourful flower borders. **Hyde Park** and **Kensington Gardens** offer a variety of trees, flowers and shrubberies, which even extend

RIVER MANAGEMENT

Once a by-word for filth and stench, the Thames was little more than a dumping ground for everything from sewage to the effluents of Victorian factories. Recently, however, a major clean-up campaign has seen fish return to these waters, and there is also a fair amount of bird life, which is at its most prolific towards the vast Thames Estuary and in the superb London Wetlands Centre at Barnes (see p. 106). Managing the Thames is the responsibility of the Port of London Authority (PLA), which controls a 150km (93-mile) section of the river stretching from the vast Thames Estuary up to Teddington Lock.

Below: *St James's Park with Horse Guards Parade. In spring, the park is a riot of colour with white and purple crocuses.*

FREE CULTURE

London is expensive, but most major museums and galleries are now free – if this is to continue, voluntary contributions are essential, so please put something in the boxes if you can. Among the most popular freebies are the groups at South Kensington and Greenwich, the British Museum, National Gallery, National Portrait Gallery, both Tates, Imperial War Museum, Museum of London, Museum of Garden History, Photographers Gallery, Wallace Collection, Kenwood House and Sir John Soane's Museum.

Below: *A fallow deer buck in Richmond Park, one of London's wildlife havens.*

along busy Park Lane. **Battersea Park**, south of the river, features blooming cherry and acacia in the spring. **Richmond Park** in southwest London is renowned for its magnificent oak trees, as well as thickets of flowering rhododendrons. For plant lovers London's main Mecca is, of course, the wonderful **Royal Botanic Gardens** at Kew, a World Heritage site where greenhouses contain everything from towering palms and epiphytes to climbers and sacred lotus plants. One of the greatest storehouses in the world for plants of all kinds, Kew has magnificent displays (*see* p. 109).

Wildlife

London has a surprising variety of birdlife, even though in many areas all you see are pigeons, blackbirds and starlings. The parks are home to numerous species, many of them introduced. The Serpentine in Hyde Park, for instance, is a fishing ground for tufted ducks, mallards, great crested grebes, moorhens, coots, and herons. In spring, migrant birds such as willow warblers, redstarts and spotted flycatchers are often seen in the parks' woodlands. Grey squirrels (introduced from North America) are fairly ubiquitous too. The largest of the royal parks, Richmond, is home to kestrels, great spotted woodpeckers, nuthatches and other bird species, as well as deer (*see* p. 110).

Once so polluted that nothing could live in it, the Thames has been cleaned up and fish have started to recolonize it. Blackheaded, common and herring gulls may be seen dipping in it as they fish, and along the more rural areas upstream the kingfisher is in evidence as are elegant swans (protected for centuries as Crown property). The Thames Estuary and the London Wetlands Centre (*see* p. 106) are important habitats for migrating birds during the winter months.

HISTORY IN BRIEF

The Thames Valley was home to hunter-gatherers some 500,000 years ago, and although there were isolated settlements by the time of the **Celts** it was not until the arrival of the **Romans** that a larger, more permanent settlement was founded.

Londinium to Lundenwic

In AD43 an invasion force of four Roman legions sailed from Boulogne, landing at Richborough in Kent and overwhelming the Celtic forces along the way before building a pontoon bridge across the Thames (probably near present-day Westminster) to push further northwards. Their goal was the powerful tribal stronghold of Camulodunum (Colchester), which, once conquered, became the Roman capital.

In AD60 a major rebellion by the **Iceni** tribes, under **Queen Boudicca** (Boadicea), led to the sacking of Camulodunum and a massacre of the inhabitants of the river crossing at **Londinium**. After the defeat of the Iceni (and Boudicca's suicide) Londinium was rebuilt as the main Roman base in Britain. The port prospered and grew to become the fifth most important city in the Roman Empire until the withdrawal of the Romans in the 5th century AD.

During the 6th century the settlement – then known as **Lundenwic** – prospered once more under the Anglo-Saxons, and became a thriving port until being razed to the ground by the **Vikings** in AD851. Some 30 years later the English, led by King Alfred the Great, recaptured London, but by 1016 it had again fallen to the Danes.

The death of pious **Edward the Confessor** – who founded Westminster Abbey – in 1066, was soon followed by the invasion of **William the Conqueror**, who laid the foundations for the Tower of London and Windsor Castle. London's special status was reaffirmed by the election of its first **mayor** in the 12th century.

Above: *The statue of Queen Boudicca at Westminster, a reminder of London's Roman past.*

GEOFFREY CHAUCER

Born into a family of London vintners, poet **Geoffrey Chaucer** (c. 1342–1400) travelled widely in his many jobs – he was at various times a diplomat, customs official, member of parliament and a soldier – and the wide range of people he met contributed to his great knowledge of human nature, which was expounded to such good effect in *The Canterbury Tales*. This rollicking saga of pilgrims on the road to Canterbury was one of the first books to be printed and the first major work of literature in the English language.

The Middle Ages

By the 14th century London's population had reached around 80,000 people but the **Black Death** (1348) wiped out over a third of the population. Economic unrest led to the **Peasant's Revolt** of 1381, a protest at the imposition of the poll tax in which Londoners opened their gates to the rebels (under Wat Tyler) and joined in the ransacking of palaces and merchants' houses.

Throughout the 15th century trade with other countries continued to expand, and the wharfs around **London Bridge** were stacked high with cargo such as wines, spices, furs, and imported cloth. Literacy was on the increase and in 1476 **William Caxton** returned from Bruges with the first printing press, which he set up at Westminster. He published over 90 books (including an edition of *The Canterbury Tales*) before his death, after which his assistant Wynkyn de Worde moved his presses to the Fleet Street district, establishing the beginnings of the printing and publishing trade in the area which was to last for several centuries.

Tudors and Stuarts

With the defeat of Richard III by Henry VII in the **Wars of the Roses**, the House of Tudor established a long-lasting peace, during which London became a centre for world commerce, with the opening up of trade routes to the Orient and the discovery of America. During the reign of **Henry VIII** the Royal Navy was established and the Church of England split from Rome – the **Reformation**, as it was known, was instigated by the king, who wanted to divorce his first wife, Catherine of Aragon. During the Dissolution of the Monasteries (1536) which followed, scores of churches and monasteries in the capital were ransacked; many were then converted to secular use by the Tudor nobility.

ELIZABETHAN THEATRE

The 'golden age' of the Elizabethan era led to the flowering of literature and drama and the rise of playwrights and authors such as William Shakespeare, Ben Jonson and Christopher Marlowe. Theatre performances took place on temporary stages outside pubs, and were looked down upon by the city fathers as degenerate. James Burbage then constructed London's first theatre in Shoreditch, outside the City boundaries, in 1574. Later, he dismantled it to create the **Globe** in Southwark (see p. 97), where Shakespeare's plays were first performed. The Globe has now been recreated, albeit not on the original site.

Henry VIII built a new palace, **St James's**, seized **Hampton Court** from his former chancellor, Thomas Wolsey, and established numerous hunting areas which are today London's Royal Parks: Hyde Park, Regent's Park, Richmond Park and Greenwich Park.

Under **Elizabeth I** the country enjoyed considerable prosperity, and the establishment of the city's first trading centre, the **Royal Exchange** (built by Sir Thomas Gresham in 1567), helped shift the balance of commercial power in Europe from Antwerp to London. The establishment of joint-stock companies (such as the Levant Company, Hudson Bay Company and East India Company) facilitated the exploits of seafarers and traders such as Walter Raleigh, Francis Drake and John Hawkins. By 1600 London had grown to encompass a population of around 200,000 people.

The Tudor dynasty ended in 1603 with the death of Elizabeth I. She was succeeded by James VI of Scotland, who united the two countries for the first time, becoming James I of England and VI of Scotland. The continued persecution of Catholics led to the **Gunpowder Plot** on 5 November 1605, when Guy Fawkes and his fellow conspirators were caught in the act of trying to blow up the Houses of Parliament in protest.

Under James I's son, Charles I, the Crown found itself at odds with Parliament and the City and tensions increased when the king tried (unsuccessfully) to arrest five Members of Parliament in 1642: this sparked a **Civil War** with the Royalists pitched against the Parliamentarians under Oliver Cromwell. The Royalists lost, and Charles I was executed outside the Banqueting House in Whitehall on 30 January 1649.

For the next 11 years England became a Republic under Oliver Cromwell, until the **Restoration** of the monarchy under Charles II in 1660.

In 1665, London was hit by an outbreak of the **bubonic plague**, and the following year another major disaster occurred when the **Great Fire** of 1666 destroyed large areas of the city (*see* p. 74); it did, however, wipe out the last remnants of the plague.

THE PLAGUE

As London expanded, conditions became increasingly unsanitary: the Thames was not only the main highway and water supply, but also the main dumping ground for sewage and effluents from the tanning, brewing and soap industries. There were outbreaks of **bubonic plague** (carried by fleas living on black rats) in 1603, 1625, 1636 and 1647, but a long, hot summer in 1665 led to an epidemic which killed around 100,000 inhabitants of the city.

Opposite: *The White Tower is at the centre of the great medieval castle of the Tower of London.* **Below:** *Staple Inn in Holborn, one of the few timber-framed buildings to survive the Great Fire.*

CHOLERA OUTBREAKS

As the city expanded during the 19th century it was increasingly beset by health problems. Most of the population depended on street pumps for their water supplies, but the water supplied came mostly from the Thames – which was itself a dumping ground for sewage from the capital. In 1832, a cholera epidemic broke out, with a second outbreak in 1848–9. In 1858 a long, hot summer reduced water levels in the Thames until it was little more than a running sewer, and parliament was forced to go into recess because of the 'Great Stink'. The problem was finally addressed by the newly created Metropolitan Board of Works whose chief engineer, Sir Joseph Bazalgette, built a series of embankments along the Thames and eliminated the foul-smelling mud-flats.

Charles II wanted to reconstruct London along continental lines, with grand boulevards and circuses, but the intricacies of property ownership rendered this impractical. Many streets were, however, considerably widened as rebuilding went ahead – and bricks and mortar replaced the wooden houses of medieval London.

Georgian London

In 1714 the throne passed to George of Hanover, who became **George I** but never learned to speak English. Parliament gained in stature and the leader of the Whigs (Liberals), Sir Robert Walpole, effectively became the first Prime Minister. The king presented him with **No. 10 Downing Street**, which has been the Prime Minister's residence ever since. Tony Blair has broken this tradition.

London continued to grow, and numerous Georgian-style squares and terraces were built in Soho, Bloomsbury, Marylebone and Mayfair. The **West End** was developed as a fashionable shopping area, but squalor and poverty were also on the increase. The **East End** saw considerable deprivation and appallingly high death rates – the latter particularly fuelled by a glut of cheap gin, consumed at the rate of around two pints per week by adults and children alike. In 1751, Parliament

was forced to raise the price of gin to try and halt the epidemic. The imbalance between the rich and the poor led to high crime rates – daylight robbery in the West End was not unknown – and an increasing number of riots, one of the most serious of which was the **Gordon Riots** of 1780, which lasted for five days and led to over 300 deaths.

The 19th Century

In 1801, when the first official census was taken, London's population stood at around one million inhabitants, making it the most populous city in Europe. Over the next century it grew to nearly seven million as the city became increasingly industrialized and developed as the commercial and administrative hub of the British Empire. In

1811 the Prince Regent (later King George IV), laid out plans for Regent's Park and Regent Street with architect John Nash; the British Museum was begun in 1823, the National Gallery in 1824, and London University was founded in 1826.

During the reign of **Queen Victoria**, roads, railways and houses continued to be built right across the capital, and docks were developed on the banks of the Thames. Pollution, squalor, prostitution and overcrowding were endemic in the slumlands of the East End; this was the underbelly of prosperous Victorian society which was so effectively chronicled by Charles Dickens.

The city's first railway line (from London Bridge to Greenwich) was opened in 1836, and the first underground line (between Paddington and Farringdon Road) was built in 1863. The achievements of the Victorian era were celebrated in the **Great Exhibition** (*see* p. 59) of 1851, an event which was so successful (attracting over six million visitors) that it led Prince Albert, the Queen's Consort, to establish an 'arts and science metropolis' – the foundation of today's museums in South Kensington.

Above: *Cumberland Terrace, in Regent's Park, is an elegant example of Nash architecture.*
Opposite: *Downing Street has been the residence of Prime Ministers since the mid 18th century.*

London at War

At the outbreak of **World War I** in August 1914 the crowds cheered the troops off to war, but the patriotic euphoria was short-lived as it became apparent that it was not going to be 'all over by Christmas'. The first bombs (dropped from a Zeppelin) fell on Stoke Newington in May 1915, but casualties in the capital were slight compared to the mortality rate and the horrors of the trenches in Belgium and northern France.

EDWARDIAN DECADENCE

The turn of the century in London was marked by the decadent Edwardian era, with flamboyant fashions and music halls enlivening the city after the dour Victorian years. The Ritz, Harrods, the Café Royal, Whiteleys and Selfridges opened for business, and the first motor cars were seen on the streets of the capital. Motor buses gradually replaced the horse-drawn variety, and electric trams were introduced.

Above: *The Map Room, one of the Cabinet War Rooms where Churchill and his Cabinet held meetings during World War II.*

THE BLITZ

During the Blitz, the Luftwaffe bombed the capital for 57 consecutive nights, and Londoners sought shelter in the underground stations or purpose-built shelters in their gardens. Firemen and thousands of volunteers fought bravely to contain the fires and rescue those buried in the rubble of their houses. The worst night came on 29 December 1940, when thousands of incendiary bombs threatened to set the capital alight. By the end of the Blitz, in May 1941, over a third of the City and the East End lay in ruins; over 30,000 people had died, with 50,000 injured and 130,000 houses destroyed.

In the inter-war years London's population continued to expand. The greatest growth was in the newly created suburbs, particularly to the north. The voting franchise was extended to all males over 21 years of age and females over 30, although it was not until 1928 that universal suffrage was achieved. Previously the vote had been restricted to the landed gentry, middle-class professionals, and 'settled tenants' (workers in towns).

In an attempt to emulate the success of the Great Exhibition, the British Empire Exhibition was held at Wembley in 1924–5, but its displays of the wealth and might of the Empire were overshadowed by a looming Depression. A confrontation between mine-owners and the unions led to the **General Strike** of 1926, with London in a state of near anarchy for nine days until the strike leaders caved in.

At the outbreak of **World War II** in 1939 trench shelters were dug in London's parks, over 600,000 women and children were evacuated to the countryside, and the strict enforcement of night-time blackouts led to a huge increase in road accidents. But the bombs didn't arrive for another year, with the beginning of the **Blitz** in September 1940, marked by many deaths and thousands injured.

Postwar Years

Victory in Europe (VE) Day, in 1945, was followed by a General Election, where Winston Churchill was defeated by Clement Attlee's Labour Party. The Welfare State was created and the government embarked on wholesale nationalization of key industries. But in the capital the most pressing problem was a shortage of houses: prefabricated buildings were erected all over the city and massive high-rise housing estates were built on derelict bomb sites. In an attempt to relieve the austerity of day-to-day life, the **Festival of Britain** was staged in 1951 on the south bank of the Thames; the site eventually became the South Bank Centre.

During the 1950s the population of the capital fell, although there was also a large influx of immigrants from the former colonies and the Caribbean. The '**Swinging Sixties**' heralded a new era of liberation and 'groovy' London became the music and fashion capital of the world.

The 1970s seemed drab by comparison, with economic austerity leading to the three-day week in 1974 and the downfall of the Conservative government. Britain became part of the EEC, and the IRA started a long bombing campaign on the mainland. At the end of the 1970s **Margaret Thatcher** swept to power and began a process of privatization and cuts in public services which was to leave few areas untouched.

In 1990, riots in Trafalgar Square against the poll tax helped see off the deeply unpopular Maggie Thatcher but it wasn't until May 1997 that growing dissatisfaction with Conservative rule led to the election of Tony Blair's Labour Party. They were re-elected with ease in 2001 but the 2005 elections were marked by growing dissatisfaction with Blair's handling of the Iraq war.

New structures marking London's transition into the 21st century include the Millennium Dome, the conversion of a power station into Tate Modern and the innovative Millenium Bridge. The newest major addition to London's skyline is the Swiss Re Tower (commonly known as 'The Gherkin'). Projects currently in progress include the re-development of King's Cross into a gateway for Eurostar and a reshaping of large areas of East London in preparation for the 2012 Olympics.

LONDON FACTS

London has:
- four World Heritage sites;
- nearly 900 conservation areas;
- 147 registered parks and gardens and 8 royal parks;
- urban public parks covering 30% of the city;
- 83 street markets and 10 farmers' markets;
- over 150 theatres, about 50 of which are in the West End;
- over 100 arts events every day;
- twice as many museums as Paris or New York;
- around 7000 licensed restaurants, 36 of which have Michelin stars; cuisine from around 80 Countries;
- nearly 4000 pubs;
- over 300 after-midnight venues, including 233 nightclubs and 23 casinos;
- 21,000 licensed taxis

Below: *The controversial Millennium Dome at Greenwich, a multi-million-pound structure that will be a venue for the 2012 Olympics.*

GOVERNING LONDON

The first step towards the creation of a governing body – the mark of a true city – was the establishment of the Metropolitan Board of Works in 1855, which administered services such as street mainte-nance, sewerage and lighting. In 1888, the London County Council (LCC) became the first elected ruling body and was responsible for building County Hall, its neoclassical headquarters (completed in 1920), opposite the Houses of Parliament.

London now has 31 boroughs (plus the Cities of Westminster and London) and each has its own Lord Mayor (primarily a ceremonial post), of which the best known is the 'Lord Mayor of London' – actually the Lord Mayor of the City of London. The post of 'Mayor of London', of which Ken Livingstone is the first incumbent, is an administra-tive job that covers the whole of the capital.

GOVERNMENT AND ECONOMY

The UK is a constitutional monarchy, with the seat of government based in London. Britain has no written constitution and theoretically the Queen has the power to veto legislation, although her approval for new laws nowadays is more of a formality than anything else. The government of the day is led by the Prime Minister and his Cabinet of key ministers, who place legislation before Parliament for ratification. Sitting in the Palace of Westminster, Parliament consists of the 659 elected Members of the House of Commons and the unelected House of Lords. The latter came under fire as an anachronism and some hereditary peers were ousted, but qualifications to sit in the new Lords have yet to be agreed, and the number of 'Tony's cronies' receiving peerages has caused even greater controversy.

Local Government

In 1965, the London County Council was replaced by the **Greater London Council** (GLC), which controlled the entire 1580km² (610 sq miles) of Greater London and was responsible for a wide range of services and strategic planning. The GLC found itself at odds with central Government, a situation which reached its peak under the socialist GLC leader, 'Red Ken' Livingstone, in the 1980s. The GLC's introduction of subsidized public trans-port policies was anathema to the Thatcher government, who responded by abolishing the GLC in 1986. In May 1998, however, a referendum decided that Greater London should have an elected mayor and its own assembly, responsible for transport, fire, police and other services. Ironically the subsequent mayoral elections (in 2000 and 2004) put 'Red Ken' back in power.

Economy

London continues to dominate in the political and financial arenas and leads the UK in many other areas including the arts, culture, fashion, publishing, retailing, the media and much else besides. Tourism is an impor-tant component of the economy, with nearly 30 million

annual visitors. Although London is home to just 13% of the UK's population, it accounts for 18% of GDP (Gross Domestic Product); the GDP per capita is 28% higher than the national average.

Service industries make up the largest share of the metropolitan economy, with the concentration of financial, professional and business services reflecting the city's international role. But manufacturing still accounts for 9% of London's GDP. Pharmaceutical and medical research are also strong.

The capital is the UK's centre of higher education and among the world's centres for international finance, diplomacy, equity training, publishing, medical and scientific research, arbitration, media and creative industries.

London is the longest established of the world's primary financial centres, and is the world's largest centre for foreign exchange trading, international bank lending, derivatives, reinsurance and Eurobonds. Most of Europe's top law firms have offices in the city, reflecting the importance of London as a centre for international arbitration. As a centre for media and creative industries, it also has around a quarter of Europe's top 100 media companies.

London's standing as a global centre for international business may be enhanced as Britain integrates more fully into Europe.

Above: *The skyline of the City of London, a mosaic of modern architecture, is very impressive at night.*
Opposite: *The gilded statue of Justice sits atop the Old Bailey, or Central Criminal Court.*
Below: *The sumptuous interior of the stately House of Lords.*

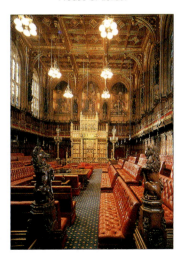

Above: *The annual Notting Hill Carnival.*

THE PEOPLE

For centuries London has been a cosmopolitan city, attracting people from other nations to live and work here. Refugees, traders, artists and others over the generations have flocked to what John Milton dubbed the 'mansion-house of liberty'. Today you will find not only the Irish (during the 19th century there were already over 100,000 Irish in London), Italians, Bangladeshis, Germans and West Indians but also Kurds, Somalis, Moroccans, Portuguese and people from every corner of the globe. More than a quarter of London's 7.2 million residents belong to a minority ethnic group and there are no less than 50 non-indigenous communities, i.e. communities of over 10,000 people who were born outside the UK and now live in the capital.

It is estimated that over 250 languages are spoken in the city and it is claimed that around 30% of Londoners are immigrants. Writer HV Morton concluded in the 1940s that 'one of the charms of London is that there are no Londoners', while Evelyn Waugh bewailed the fact that 'The English are already hard to find in London. No-one lives there who is not paid to do so … I believe that London society has ceased to exist.'

Ethnic London

London is by no means a homogenous entity and Londoners tend to associate more with the neighbour-hoods in which they live than with the city as a whole. There are no 'ghettos' as such, although immigrant groups have tended to settle in certain localities for particular reasons: Punjabi Sikhs, for instance, populated Southall in the vicinity of Heathrow Airport because it was near their point of arrival, and the airport offered work. Cypriots gravitated to Camden and Finsbury, where they could use their skills in the clothing trade, while Bengali Muslims moved to the area around Brick Lane in Tower Hamlets for similar reasons. The Chinese, too, moved into the East End – but, curiously, it was the introduction of public launderettes which largely put paid to their traditional laundry businesses and precipitated a switch to running

Chinese restaurants in Soho. The Afro-Caribbean community has traditionally been based in Brixton, to the south of the river, and Notting Hill, west of the centre.

London Neighbourhoods

While the 1960s witnessed some breaking down of the rigid class barriers of London society, Londoners still tend to be seen as haughty, snobbish and unfriendly by those who live in the provinces, and the smart districts – Mayfair, Knightsbridge, and Kensington – are still largely the preserve of the wealthy elite, while the East End is a steadfastly working class area. Meanwhile, from the 1970s onwards, the professional classes recolonized great swathes of North London – from Hampstead to Hackney – as well as areas south of the Thames (such as Camberwell and Greenwich) and property prices soared as gentrification led to a proliferation of wine bars, delicatessens and the like alongside the renovation of 19th-century terraces. During the 1980s the upwardly mobile 'yuppies' extended this process to Docklands, converting old warehouses into stylish 'loft apartments' and parking their Porsches in the shadow of long-defunct dockyard cranes.

Londoners tend to associate more with their locality or neighbourhood than might be imagined, venturing forth for shopping and entertainment to the West End or to the City and elsewhere to work. The City itself is a curious anomaly: formerly the heart of London, it has a resident population of only a little over 7000, but the daytime population soars to over 300,000 as the commuters arrive.

It may be romanticizing the cohesion of local communities too much to claim that London is a collection of villages, but architecturally and otherwise the vestiges are still there in places such as

COCKNEYS

A 'Cockney' in the broadest sense is anyone born and bred in London, although it usually applies only to working class East End residents – traditionally, only those born within the sound of the bells of St Mary-le-Bow in Cheapside. Cockney rhyming slang thrives in street markets and pubs: 'tit for tat' is a hat, 'apples and pears' are the stairs, and so on. Cockney 'Pearly Kings and Queens' put on their traditional, button-studded costumes for the Costermongers Pearly Harvest Festival Service held at the church of St Martin-in-the-Fields (Trafalgar Square) on the first Sunday in October every year. A 'costermonger' is someone who sells fruit and other produce from a market barrow, and this is essentially a harvest festival.

Below: *Pearly Kings and Queen in traditional regalia.*

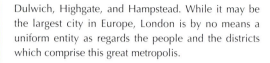

SPORTING VENUES

Tickets for major international sporting events can be extremely hard to come by, and you need to book well in advance (sometimes several months). Here are some useful telephone numbers:
• Ascot Racecourse,
tel: (0870) 727 1234;
• Crystal Palace National Sports Centre,
tel: (020) 8778 0131;
• Epsom Downs,
tel: (01372) 726 311;
• Kempton Park,
tel: (01932) 782 292;
• Lord's Cricket Ground,
tel: (020) 7289 1611;
• Sandown Park,
tel: (01372) 464 348;
• The Oval,
tel: (020) 7582 6660;
• Twickenham Stadium,
tel: (0870) 405 2000;
• Wembley Stadium, tel: (020) 8795 9000;
• Wimbledon All England Lawn Tennis Club,
tel: (020) 8944 1066;
• Windsor,
tel: (0870) 220 0024

Dulwich, Highgate, and Hampstead. While it may be the largest city in Europe, London is by no means a uniform entity as regards the people and the districts which comprise this great metropolis.

Sport and Recreation

Whether you want to spectate or to become involved, there are numerous opportunities to participate in sporting activities in and around London. Many top international fixtures take place in the hallowed grounds of sporting venues such as **Lord's** (cricket), **Wimbledon** (tennis), **Crystal Palace** (athletics), **Wembley Stadium** (football), and **Twickenham** (Rugby Union). In addition, world-famous horse races take place at locations such as **Ascot**, **Epsom**, and **Sandown Park**.

For those who want to do more than just watch, London offers opportunities for the sporty to take part in all sorts of activities, ranging from aerobics to windsurfing. Council-run facilities provide inexpensive access to sports such as tennis, swimming, weight-training, aerobics and so on. There are also numerous private gymnasiums and health clubs, including some in major hotels. London's parks, of course, offer opportunities for jogging, walking, tennis, boating or swimming.

Athletics: Major international events, as well as local contests, take place at the **Crystal Palace National Sports Centre**, with the two biggest competitions in summer: June/July and July/August.

Cricket: The cricket season runs from April to September. England's love of cricket is best appreciated on a sunny weekend afternoon, from a traditional pub overlooking the village green. Although dominated by arcane rules and peculiar terminology ('silly mid-offs', 'yorkers', 'googlies' and so on), the game can arouse fierce rivalry. The biggest drawcards of the season are the international **test matches** between England and touring teams, one of which is always played at **Lord's Cricket Ground** (the home of the Middlesex County

Cricket Club) in St John's Wood, and another at **The Oval** in Kennington.

Football: Football (soccer) probably arouses more passion in the English than any other game, and although it is usually the big northern clubs which dominate the league tables, London prides itself on the strength of its teams such as Arsenal (the Gunners), Tottenham Hotspur (Spurs) and Chelsea. The season is from mid-August to early May, culminating in the FA Cup Final at Wembley Stadium.

Horse Racing: A day at the races provides an entertaining insight into the personalities of the British people from all walks of life, with a flutter on the filly of your choice adding excitement to the occasion. Major race courses within easy reach of London include **Ascot**

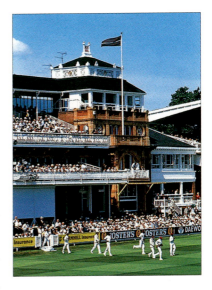

(with the highlight being the glamorous Royal Ascot meeting in June), **Epsom** (one of the world's fastest courses, home to Derby Day in June), **Kempton Park** (where meetings are far less snobby than elsewhere), **Sandown Park** (popular for day trips from the capital), and **Windsor** (which has a delightful setting alongside the Thames).

Above: *Lord's Cricket Ground, in St John's Wood, is one of London's most famous sporting venues.*
Opposite: *Around 46,000 people take part in the annual London Marathon.*

Rugby: There are two kinds of rugby (or rugger) played in Britain, **Rugby Union** (15-a-side) and **Rugby League** (13-a-side). In London there is one Rugby League team (the London Broncos), with other major teams (such as the Wasps, Harlequins and London Irish) playing Rugby Union. The season runs from September to April/May, culminating in the **Pilkington Cup** (the equivalent of the FA Cup Final), held at the end of April at the modern and impressive **Twickenham Stadium** in West London.

Tennis: A climax of the international tennis season is the Grand Slam championship tournament, played on the famous grass courts at **Wimbledon** during the last week of June and the first week of July. Almost as famous for the cost of off-court strawberries as for the

Right: *Wimbledon is the setting for the prestigious lawn tennis championship: one of the sport's four Grand Slam events.*

on-court antics of the international stars, tickets for the 'Wimbledon fortnight' are notoriously hard to obtain.

The Arts

Architecture: The only vestiges of **Roman** Londinium are parts of the old Roman wall (visible at Tower Hill) and the ruins of the Temple of Mithras. **Norman** buildings are represented by the Tower of London and the church of St Bartholomew the Great in Smithfield, and the undercroft of Westminster Abbey. Most of the Abbey was rebuilt from the 13th century onwards in the **Medieval Gothic** style, other examples of which include Southwark Cathedral. The **Tudor** style tended to favour red brick over stone, with the most outstanding examples being Hampton Court Palace and St James's Palace.

The **English Renaissance** is best exemplified by the work of Inigo Jones, responsible for the Queen's House at Greenwich, the Banqueting House at Westminster, and the piazza in Covent Garden. The other great architect of the era was Sir Christopher Wren: following the Great Fire in 1666, Wren rebuilt St Paul's Cathedral and no less than 51 other churches in the City, as well as the Old Royal Observatory at Greenwich, the Royal Hospital in Chelsea, and numerous other landmarks. During the 18th century the **neoclassical** style was fashionable, when designer Robert Adam remodelled mansions such as Kenwood House, Osterley Park and Syon House. It was during this period that John Nash laid out Regent Street, linking St James's Palace with Regent's Park. The legacy of the **Georgian** period can be seen in the numerous elegant terraced houses which still exist in areas such as Bloomsbury, Islington, Greenwich, Dulwich and Hampstead.

During the **Victorian** era London was transformed by the building of new roads, railways, bridges, canals and docks. Prestigious buildings of this period (some harking back to the neoclassical or even Gothic traditions) include the British Museum, the Houses of Parliament, the National Gallery, Tower Bridge, the Natural History Museum and St Pancras Station. **Edwardian** London gave us the Old Bailey and department stores such as Whiteleys, Selfridges and Harrods. The city has few buildings from the **Modernist** era, and although there were once scores of Art Deco cinemas, most have now been demolished.

The **Postwar** period saw the building of the Royal Festival Hall, the unusual Commonwealth Institute, and dozens of concrete tower blocks (many of which are now being pulled down). Concrete also predominated in the construction of the South Bank Complex and the Barbican Centre complex.

Most **post-Modernist** architecture has been concentrated in the City and Docklands, notable structures including Lloyd's of London, the Canary Wharf tower, the Broadgate development next to Liverpool Street Station, the London Ark in Hammersmith, Waterloo International Terminal, the new British Library, the Channel 4 Television building, the Millennium Dome, the Millennium Bridge and Tate Modern. One of the newest buildings in the City is the Swiss Re Tower.

Art: For the art lover, London offers not only some of the world's greatest collections of Western art but also a thriving contemporary scene with a huge range of new, creative talent

THE LONDON PASS

Whether a tourist pass saves you money depends on what you plan to do, especially as many of the major museums and galleries are now free (*see* p. 8) – but it is worth looking into.

What is available changes, but a major one that has been around for some time is **The London Pass**, giving free admission to over 50 sights plus various discounts over 1, 2, 3 or 6 days. For information, tel: (01664) 485 020 or visit www.londonpass.com – if the pass is purchased through the web, it includes a Travelcard.

Below: *Swiss Re Tower, usually called the Gherkin.*

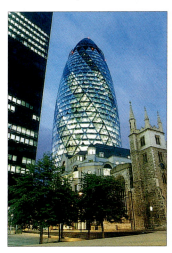

THEATRE TOURS

If you want to find out more about what goes on in some of London's famous theatres, you can take backstage tours (from 30 to 75 minutes) of several major theatres including the National Theatre (although it is officially 'Royal', nobody ever refers to it as such), South Bank Centre, tel: (020) 7452 3400 (tours), 7452 3000 (box office); and the Theatre Royal, Drury Lane, Catherine St, WC2, tel: (0870) 890 1109. Numbers are limited, so it's sensible to book in advance.

BRIGHT LIGHTS, BIG CITY

The quality and variety of London's arts, culture and entertainment scene is probably unrivalled anywhere in the world. To navigate your way around this cultural maze, the most comprehensive listings of what's on are found in the weekly *Time Out*, and *What's On*. Alternatively, there are comprehensive listings at www.visitlondon.com

on display. The historic collections that can be seen in the National Gallery, Tate Britain, Tate Modern, Courtauld Institute, British Museum and Victoria and Albert Museum provide sufficient riches to sustain even the most ardent enthusiast.

In modern art, London has a number of dynamic young artists (names to watch out for include Damien Hirst, Helen Chadwick, Mat Collishaw, Fiona Rae and Anya Gallacio, amongst others) whose work can often be seen – for free – in the **commercial galleries** of Dering and Cork streets, both in the West End. The **Summer Exhibition** at the Royal Academy mostly features amateur artists, but the usually controversial **Turner Prize** exhibits, which are displayed at Tate Britain in the month preceding the judging (November), are worth seeing. Another avenue to explore is the summer **degree shows** held at the various London art colleges in late May/June, in particular those at Goldsmiths, the Royal College, the Royal Academy, the Slade, and St Martin's School of Art.

Theatre: With a stage history that dates back to the father of theatre, William Shakespeare, it is little wonder that London is often considered the theatre capital of the world. While the West End may appear to be dominated by blockbusting musicals, numerous other stages provide the platform for inventive, talented work and original productions. London's South Bank is home to the **National Theatre** and stars of both stage and screen can be seen in many West End productions. In addition, there's a thriving **fringe theatre** scene, with avant-garde plays staged in locations as diverse as pubs and converted warehouses. On most days you can choose from over 100 live shows.

Cinema: With 95 cinemas offering 500 screens, there's no shortage of choice, both art-house and Hollywood blockbusters being easy to find – along with plenty of foreign-language movies and documentaries.

Classical Music, Opera and Dance: London has a number of venues for classical music, ranging from the ornate splendour of the **Royal Albert Hall** to the three, purpose-built halls of the **South Bank Centre**, the acoustically perfect **Wigmore Hall**, and the **Barbican Centre** com-

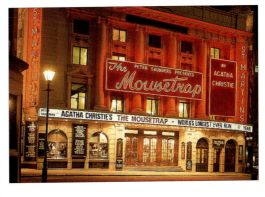

plex, and on any one day there are likely to be several performances to choose from. The capital is home to the **Royal Philharmonic Orchestra**, the **London Symphony Orchestra**, the **London Philharmonic Orchestra**, the **Philharmonia**, and the **BBC Symphony Orchestra**, to name but the most prominent. Concerts are, in many cases, poorly attended (to the shame of Londoners), so there is rarely a problem getting tickets. You can take advantage of free **lunchtime concerts** from Monday to Friday in many churches (such as St Martin-in-the-Fields, St James's Church in Piccadilly, and several others). Outdoor concerts are also held at **Kenwood House** in the summer (see p. 89); a wide range of works is also performed during the **Henry Wood Promenade Concerts**, '**The Proms**', (see p. 67) during the summer months.

Opera was first staged at the **Royal Opera House** in 1817, and performances still pack the house despite the exorbitant ticket prices. More reasonably priced performances can be seen at the **London Coliseum**, home to the **English National Opera**. New and innovative works are often performed during the Jun–Jul **Almeida Opera Festival** at the **Almeida Theatre** in Islington (see p. 90).

There are nearly 50 major **rock and pop** venues (including Astoria, Barfly, Forum, Garage and Marquee) and over 50 central night clubs.

Above: *Popular theatre productions can run for decades. The Mousetrap is the longest running play in the world.*
Opposite: *Salvador Dalí's surreal version of a love seat; the Mae West Lips Sofa, on view at Dalí Universe (see p. 96).*

JAZZ

Jazz is easy to find, notably at Ronnie Scott's Club, 47 Frith Street, tel: (020) 7439 0747, www.ronniescotts.co.uk. Established in 1959, this is the acknowledged home of London jazz and all the greats have played here. 'Real' membership is expensive, but you can get one night's membership at the door. Booking's advisable: essential if you don't like standing. Or try The 100 Club, 100 Oxford Street, tel: (020) 7636 0933 (booking unnecessary).

Above: *Tea at the Ritz is a British institution.*

Dance in all its varied forms is well represented in the capital, with every style from the classic showpieces of the **Royal Ballet** to contemporary works and even Brazilian or Indian dance on display. Major venues include the **ICA**, the **London Coliseum**, the **Royal Opera House**, **Riverside Studios** (Hammersmith), and the **South Bank Centre**. In addition, regional and international touring companies often perform in London. One of the best showcases for new talent is the annual **Dance Umbrella** festival, held in October/November.

AFTERNOON TEA

Afternoon tea is another great British institution which shouldn't be missed. Mostly the speciality of the grand hotels, the set tea usually involves 'finger' sandwiches (smoked salmon, cucumber and the like) followed by assorted cakes, scones with clotted cream and strawberry jam and other assorted cakes/pastries – with, of course, a good choice of teas. Most of the big hotels have dress codes (no jeans or trainers). The Ritz requires bookings weeks in advance. For the Savoy a week is usually sufficient. Be prepared to dig deep: about £35 a head.

Food and Drink

British food may once have been something of an international joke, epitomized by things like comforting, stodgy pies and puddings ('nursery food'), greasy fish and chips, and mammoth fry-ups for breakfast. But that is an image which is well past its sell-by date, particularly in London, where the range of cuisines available is huge and the variety of eateries (from pubs to trendy cafés, brasseries, wine bars, bistros and the like) has expanded enormously in recent years. Coupled with this, there has been a revolution in top-end gourmet restaurants where home-grown talent is now proving itself to be a match for the best anywhere else in the world. Whatever your budget or taste buds dictate, you can be sure that London will provide plenty of culinary adventures.

The most characteristic British drinking venue is, of course, the 'public house' or **pub**, a social institution which stretches back to the days of wayside coaching inns. London has a vast diversity of pubs, many of them dating from the Victorian era, and there are very few places where you won't find one within handy reach.

Be warned though – they can be ghastly, with plastic decor, rude staff, terrible food and gassy beer (this is particularly true in the West End, where good pubs need some ferreting out). On the other hand, the best of them will feature a good range of 'real ales' (see p. 29), a welcoming atmosphere, tasty snacks and an entertaining ambience. Many are still the centre of the surrounding communities, with 'locals' propping up the bar and socializing. Many more have also been refurbished and feature live entertainment. Good food, too, has become much more important in recent years, particularly with the rise of the 'gastropub', which combines unpretentious home cooking with the cosy warmth and neighbourliness of a typical local pub.

Most pubs have a fairly limited selection of wine so, for that, you're better off heading for a **brasserie** or **wine bar**, of which there are scores throughout the capital.

Modern British Cuisine: A new wave of restaurateurs and chefs have added spice and flair to British cuisine, proving that the capital is no longer the culinary backwater it was once thought to be – in fact, London now boasts over 30 restaurants bearing the coveted Michelin star – more than any other European city apart from Paris.

'New wave' British cuisine includes chefs such as Gordon Ramsay (Gordon Ramsay at Claridge's, Brook St, W1), Antony Worrall Thompson (at Notting Grill, Clarendon Rd, W11) Matthew Harris (at Bibendum, Fulham Rd, SW3), Jamie Oliver (at Fifteen, Westland Place, N1), and Tom Aikens (at Tom Aikens, Elystan Street, SW3) who are all presently leading the way in top British cuisine. There is no overall style to this new wave, apart from a consistent sense of inventiveness

TRADITIONAL BREAKFASTS

Traditional British breakfasts are legendary, and are usually served up to around 11:00 in hotels and cafés (some serve them all day). The obligatory fry-up of eggs, bacon, sausage and tomato is often supplemented by extras such as 'bubble and squeak', chips, baked beans, mushrooms, black pudding, kedgeree or kidneys. After one of these hearty breakfasts you'll be well set up for a day's sightseeing.

Below: *The City Barge at Strand-on-the-Green, Chiswick: one of London's many historic pubs; it dates from 1484.*

FISH AND CHIPS

Once considered to be the only worthwhile British culinary export to the world, fish and chips can be found almost everywhere – but standards vary widely. The best fish and chips are found in popular places such as the Sea Shell (in Lisson Grove) and Geale's (at Notting Hill Gate). There are also many excellent seafood restaurants where you can enjoy Dover sole, plaice, sea bass, or even Cockney staples such as cockles, or eel pie and mash.

Below: *Simpson's in the Strand is a good place to sample traditional roast beef.*

and an eclectic use of ingredients and methods which draws on everything from West Coast/Californian to Mediterranean and Far Eastern influences.

Entertaining Themes: Another recent phenomenon on the London restaurant scene has been the rise of mega entertainment and eating venues, pioneered by style guru Sir Terence Conran with the opening of the massive 350-seat Quaglino's restaurant in 1994; in 1995 he followed this with the even bigger (700-seat) Mezzo. Meanwhile, Marco Pierre White has continued to expand his empire, which now includes the Mirabelle, the Criterion Brasserie and Quo Vadis, which is decorated with artworks by Damien Hirst. Another novel place to eat is the Floral Hall Balconies Restaurant in the recently restored Royal Opera House with its amazing glass roof. Some of the performers regularly sing at the extraordinary Sarastro restaurant in Covent Garden, which is worth visiting for the opera-related décor alone (as is its sister establishment, Papageno) – the food's not bad either.

Traditional British Food: Alongside the growth of 'modern British' cuisine (*see* p. 27), there has also been a revival of traditional cooking in the capital's restaurants, with good, hearty food thankfully banishing the excesses of nouvelle cuisine to the culinary dustbin. Some restaurants, of course, never followed fashion anyway, and places such as the 19th-century Simpson's in the Strand and the Quality Chop House (EC1) continue to serve traditional British staples, such as steak and kidney pudding and fish cakes. Bangers and mash, meat casseroles and pies, shepherd's pie, toad-in-the-hole and roast beef with Yorkshire pudding are just some of the main courses you

Left: *Hand-pumped beer is just one of the hallmarks of a traditional London pub.*

might come across. Desserts include treats such as jam roly-poly, trifles, toffee pudding, spotted dick and bread-and-butter pudding.

Ethnic Restaurants: London has always been known for its ethnic cuisine, in particular Indian, Bangladeshi and Chinese food. Many of the numerous curry houses tend to churn out identical dishes (with sauces bought in bulk) which have limited appeal, but to balance this there are many excellent establishments where freshly prepared ingredients are used to good effect in regional dishes from India, Nepal, Sri Lanka, Pakistan and Bangladesh. A similar caveat applies to Chinese restaurants, where monosodium glutamate (MSG) is heaped on regardless: however, London also has some of the best Cantonese chefs in Europe (partly due to an exodus from Hong Kong before it reverted to Chinese rule in 1997), with *dim sum* (lunchtime snacks) one of the most characteristic features of the cuisine.

The range of various ethnic restaurants does not stop there, however, and among all of these you may come across are Japanese, Korean, Thai, Malaysian, Indonesian, Turkish, Jewish, Vietnamese, Mongolian as well as different types of African and Caribbean. French, Italian and Greek are probably the most widespread of the European cuisines, but virtually all the others are represented.

REAL ALES

The classic British pub drink is a pint of **bitter**, a dark, uncarbonated brew that comes in many guises. The best bitters are those pumped by hand from the cellar, and served at room temperature. In previous decades the big breweries swallowed up many traditional small brewers and imposed a uniformly bland, gassy product on many pubs: thanks to the efforts of CAMRA (the Campaign for Real Ale) this trend was halted (if not reversed), and to taste the real thing you should avoid pubs where the beer is served by electric pump. Chilled, draught **lager** and bottled lagers are also widely available in pubs, as is Guinness, a dark, creamy Irish **stout**. The main London brewery is Fullers.

2
Whitehall and Westminster

Westminster, at the heart of the capital, has been the main seat of political and regal power for nearly a thousand years and consequently boasts some of London's most famous landmarks, such as the **Houses of Parliament**, **Big Ben** and **Westminster Abbey**. **Buckingham Palace** is nearby, as is **Trafalgar Square** with **Nelson's Column** and the **National Gallery**.

Westminster's role in the nation's history dates back to Edward the Confessor, who abandoned his predecessors' palace in the commercial heart of the city (2km/1¼ miles to the east) to build a grand church, 'West Minster', on a swampy site at the mouth of the River Tyburn, and a new palace alongside it so that he could supervise the project. The pious king died 10 days after his abbey was completed, but Westminster Palace remained as the monarch's main residence until it was damaged by fire, forcing Henry VIII to build a new one in Whitehall. The **Palace of Westminster** later became the Houses of Parliament, but Whitehall Palace burnt down in 1698, and the thoroughfare we now know as **Whitehall** – linking the Houses of Parliament with Trafalgar Square – became the preserve of government civil servants. The current Prime Minister's residence is located at **No. 11 Downing Street**.

All the area's main sights are within easy walking distance of each other, and there are connections to other parts of London along the river from Westminster Pier. Westminster itself is rather quiet – **Covent Garden** is the most lively area for food and entertainment.

DON'T MISS

*** Westminster Abbey: with its memorials embodying centuries of history.
*** Buckingham Palace: Changing of the Guard. Visit the **State Rooms** in Aug–Sep.
*** Tate Britain: British art from the 16th century to the present.
*** Trafalgar Square: see Nelson and visit the **National Gallery**.
** Clarence House: visit the charming royal residence (Aug–Sept).
** Big Ben and the **Houses of Parliament**.

Opposite: *The Houses of Parliament, 'birthplace of democracy'.*

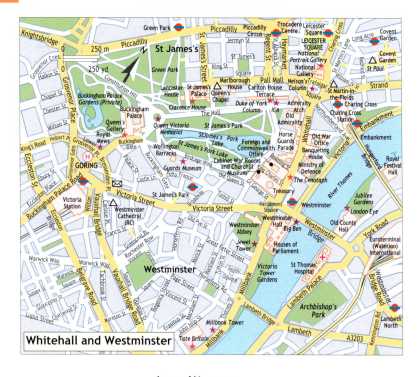

Whitehall and Westminster

ALONG WHITEHALL

This broad, 1km-long avenue links Trafalgar Square with Parliament Square, and is lined with buildings housing key government offices and ministries. It was named after the former Whitehall Palace, where Henry VIII lived for his last 14 years. The palace was destroyed by fire in 1698, and only the **Banqueting House** (open 10:00–17:00, Monday–Saturday), which was built by Inigo Jones for James I, remains. The wonderful ceiling in the main dining hall was painted by Rubens. He was commissioned by Charles I, who was put to death outside this hall in 1649. Stepping through the window on to the scaffolding outside, he wore several shirts in case he should shiver from the cold and the crowd mistake this for fear. After the execution, his head was sewn back on before the corpse was taken for burial at Windsor.

THE CHANGING OF THE GUARD AT WHITEHALL

The mounted soldiers outside **Horse Guards** are from the two Household Cavalry regiments. Those in blue and red livery belong to the Blues and Royals, while those in red tunics with white plumes belong to the Life Guards. The normal routine is in abeyance pending the construction of new stables and a **Household Cavalry Museum**, due to open in 2007.

Horse Guards *

Opposite Banqueting House is **Horse Guards**, where impassive troopers of the Queen's Household Cavalry stand guard, on foot or horseback. During the **Changing of the Guard** (*see* p. 32) mounted troopers in full livery ride up from Knightsbridge Barracks via Constitution Hill to the Horse Guards Parade, where the ceremony takes place. The **Guards Museum**, Birdcage Walk, is open daily 10:00–16:00.

Downing Street

Past the Old Treasury on the same side of Whitehall as the **Horse Guards** is the home of the British Prime Minister. No. 10 was presented to Britain's first Prime Minister, Sir Robert Walpole, in 1732, and remained the PM's residence until Tony Blair decided it was too small and took over No. 11.

Above: *The Old Admiralty faces on to the Horse Guards, the setting for the Trooping of the Colour.*

The Cenotaph *

Erected in 1919 to commemorate those whose lives were lost during World War I, the Cenotaph is the main focus of the Remembrance Sunday ceremony, which is held every November. A two-minute silence is observed for those who died in both World Wars and other conflicts.

Below: *Colourful pageantry provides a free spectacle for visitors to the city.*

Cabinet War Rooms and Churchill Museum **

Just down King Charles Street, off Whitehall's west side, are the **Cabinet War Rooms**, an underground complex which was Churchill's HQ during World War II. One section is now the **Churchill Museum**, with multimedia displays bringing the war to life. Open daily 09:30–17:00 Apr–Oct and 10:00–17:00 Nov–Mar. www.iwm.org.uk

INSIDE PARLIAMENT

If Parliament is in session at night, a light is lit at the top of Big Ben. Debates in the House of Commons take place Mon–Thu from 14:30 to late; and Fri 09:30–15:00. Visitors can watch from the Strangers Gallery by queuing at St Stephen's Gate on Parliament Square: it can take over an hour to get in. Advance tickets are needed for Prime Minister's Question Time, Wed 12:00–12:30: contact your local MP or embassy/high commission. Notes on the more arcane proceedings of the Commons are supplied. Parliament is in recess during summer (Aug to mid-Oct), when guided tours are possible.
Tel: (0870) 906 3773.

Above: *The clock-tower commonly called 'Big Ben'.*
Right: *The Houses of Parliament are an impressive sight.*

PARLIAMENT SQUARE

Laid out soon after the rebuilding of the Houses of Parliament in the mid 1800s, Parliament Square is a rather busy traffic roundabout and houses some of London's most famous landmarks, such as the Houses of Parliament, Big Ben and Westminster Abbey. There are several interesting statues dotted about Parliament Square, including those of Abraham Lincoln, Jan Smuts and a glowering Winston Churchill (in the southeast corner of the green).

Houses of Parliament ★★★

The 'Mother of all Parliaments' is one of London's best-known sights, a grandiose Victorian edifice on the north bank of the Thames which has been the site of parliamentary meetings since 1265. The 266m (872ft) riverside façade is best appreciated from Westminster Bridge, or the south bank of the Thames, with the imposing Victoria Tower to the west and the clock-tower, containing the bell known as Big Ben, to the east.

The House is divided into upper and lower houses, the **House of Commons** and the **House of Lords**. A wartime bomb destroyed the original Commons debating chamber, and reconstruction was completed in 1950. On the other side of the Central Lobby is the House of Lords, a far more splendid chamber where debates are usually less acrimonious.

Facing Parliament Square on the north side of the House is **Westminster Hall**, the only surviving relic of the original palace. Across the road from the Houses of Parliament is the 14th-century **Jewel Tower,** which now houses an exhibition on parliament's history. Open daily 10:00–17:00 Apr–Oct; 10:00–16:00 Nov–Mar. www.english-heritage.org.uk

Westminster Abbey ★★★

A masterpiece in its own right, the Abbey also presents a rich pageant of English history and has been the setting for almost every Coronation since 1066. Built on the site of a monastery in the 11th century, the present church mostly dates from the 13th century and its 30m (98ft) nave is the loftiest in the country.

It would take a whole book to describe the hundreds of memorials which fill the Abbey, but the highlights include the Tomb of the Unknown Warrior (representing all unidentifiable British servicemen who died in conflict), the Perpendicular Henry VII Chapel, the Coronation Chair, the Royal Chapels, Statesman's Corner and Poet's Corner. www.westminster-abbey.org

Above: *Westminster Abbey contains the tombs of many medieval monarchs.*

Tate Britain ★★★

Heading west from Parliament Square you reach Millbank, home to Tate Britain. The national gallery of British art from 1500 to the present day, the Tate holds the greatest collection of British art in the world. It includes works by Blake, Gainsborough, Constable, Hockney, Hogarth, Moore, and Rossetti. It also houses the renowned Turner Collection (comprising some 282 paintings and 20,000 drawings). The new Centenary Development provides additional galleries, shop and improved visitor facilities. Open daily 10:00–17:00. www.tate.org.uk

---

EXPLORING THE ABBEY

There is a charge to visit the Abbey (entrance via the north transept, expect queues in summer). Usually open 09:30–15:45 Mon–Fri (to 18:00 or 19:00 Wed), 09:30–13:45 Sat. Audio guides are available, and guided tours are offered by the Abbey's vergers – tel: (020) 7654 4900. www.westminster-abbey.org There is no separate charge to visit the Pyx Chamber, Chapter House or Museum.

Above: *Buckingham Palace is a 'must' on every tourist itinerary.* **Opposite:** *St James's Park is one of the great London parks, where you can relax on a deckchair listening to the band, feed the ducks or take a leisurely stroll.*

NASH AND THE PALACE

Buckingham House, which originally stood on this site, was the home of the Duke of Buckingham until 1762 when it was sold to George III. His successor, George IV, commissioned his favourite architect (John Nash) to expand and overhaul the house, but it wasn't until the 19-year-old Queen Victoria acceded to the throne in 1837 that it became the official Royal Palace. Nash had placed a triumphal arch in front of the palace but in 1851 this was moved to its present site in Hyde Park and is now called the Marble Arch.

ROYAL LONDON
Buckingham Palace ★★★

The official London residence of the monarch since Queen Victoria's reign, Buckingham Palace was off limits to all but a select few who were invited to the Queen's summer garden parties. The interior has been open to the public only.

Since 1993, it was decided to admit visitors to the State Apartments to help defray the costs of rebuilding Windsor Castle after a disastrous fire (*see* pp. 112–113). The Palace is only accessible during August and September (open 09:45–15:45 daily) when the Queen visits her summer retreat in Balmoral.

Entry is timed but, once in, you can proceed at your own pace. The most impressive rooms are the richly decorated Throne Room, the State Dining Room, Blue Drawing Room and Music Room. The Ballroom is the setting for investitures and entertainment, while the White Drawing Room is where the family gathers.

In the **Queen's Gallery**, changing selections from the royal art collection are on view; open daily 10:00–16:30; tel: (020) 7766 7301.

Further down Buckingham Palace Road, visit the working stables of the **Royal Mews** (open Sat–Thu 11:00–15:15 Easter–Oct; to 16:15 mid-July to mid-Sept). The original Kings Mews were pulled down to make way for Trafalgar Square, and both the new mews and Trafalgar Square were designed by **John Nash**, who was commissioned by the Prince Regent (later crowned George IV). The main attractions of the mews are the magnificent gilded and polished state carriages and coaches, in use since 1831. www.royalcollection.org.uk and www.hrp.org.uk

The Mall ★★

This broad, tree-lined boulevard sweeps down from the **Victoria Memorial** outside Buckingham Palace to the enormous **Admiralty Arch**. South of the Mall is **St James's Park**, Henry VIII's hunting reserve first opened to the public by Charles II, who liked to walk here with his mistress.

On the north side of the Mall (Buckingham Palace end), adjoining **St James's Palace**, is **Clarence House**, famed as the residence of the Queen Mother and now the London home of Prince Charles and Camilla, Duchess of Cornwall. Originally designed by John Nash for William, Duke of Clarence (hence the name), it's a charming place that reflects the taste of its more recent inhabitants. In the five rooms open to the public, such items as a table holding family photos, a bookcase containing works by P.G. Wodehouse and Dick Francis and an autographed Noel Coward songbook humanise the royals and there's a comfortable, homely atmosphere. Open daily 10:00–16:30 Aug–Sep; pre-book for guided tour, tel: (020) 7766 7303. www.royalcollection.org.uk

Past **Marlborough House** (designed by Wren) is the impressive façade of Carlton House Terrace, built by John Nash under the patronage of George IV.

From the **Duke of York Column** in the middle of the terrace there are views across St James's Park, and to the east of the steps is the entrance to the **Institute of Contemporary Art** (ICA), a trendy hangout for London's avant-garde set. The ICA has a regular and varied programme of films, talks, exhibitions and other events. The ICA Art Gallery is open 12:00–19:30, daily. www.ica.org.uk

THE CHANGING OF THE GUARD AT BUCKINGHAM PALACE

This free spectacle on the forecourt of **Buckingham Palace** still draws in the crowds as it has done for decades. The New Guard marches down from **Wellington Barracks** to arrive at the Palace just after 11:30, and the band plays while the keys are ceremonially handed over. The Old Guard then returns to the barracks, leaving the Palace in the hands of the New Guard until the following morning. The ceremony (lasting 45 mins) takes place daily Apr–Jul; alternate days Aug–Mar. It may be cancelled in wet weather.

Below: *Nelson gazes out from the top of his column.*

TRAFALGAR SQUARE

The largest non-park public area in London, Trafalgar Square formed part of architect John Nash's grand designs to transform the city in the mid-19th century. The square was named after Nelson's famous naval victory over the French in 1805, and the 51.5m (169ft) **Nelson's Column** – the focal point of the square – was finished in 1843, as was the National Gallery on its north side. The Landseer lions at the base of the column were added in 1867 and the fountains in 1936, nearly 70 years later.

On the west side of the square is the neoclassical Canada House, whose Portland Stone façade is echoed on the east side by South Africa House. The best view over Trafalgar Square is from the main entrance to the National Gallery, looking down past Nelson's Column and along the length of Whitehall to Big Ben. In the northeast corner of the square is **St Martin-in-the-Fields**, built in 1726. It has a fine Corinthian portico, topped by an unusual tower and steeple, and the interior boasts an Italian plasterwork ceiling. The crypt houses a brass-rubbing centre and a café. There are candlelit concerts at 19:30 on Thu, Fri, Sat, as well as free concerts at 13:00 on Mon, Tue and Fri. There are also jazz evenings in the crypt. www.st-martin-in-the-fields.org

In December the square is lit up by an enormous, beautifully lighted Christmas tree. A tree is donated annually by Norway in thanks to Britain for its role in the country's liberation from the Nazis during World War II.

The National Gallery ★★★

Housing one of the world's greatest permanent art collections, the National Gallery contains over 2000 paintings, including famous works of the Old Masters. The collection was begun as late as 1824 with only a few pieces, but today the scope – spanning Western Art from 1250 to around 1900 – is so enormous that it is impossible to absorb it all in one go, so use the (free) floor plan to find your favourite eras. The gallery was given a new lease of life with the opening of the five-storey Sainsbury Wing (funded by the supermarket chain) in 1991, which houses the Early Renaissance Collection. If you want to peruse the paintings chronologically, the Sainsbury Wing is the place to start. Open 10:00–18:00, Thursday–Tuesday; 10:00–21:00, Wednesday. www.nationalgallery.org.uk

The National Portrait Gallery ★★

Founded in 1856, the National Portrait Gallery houses some 10,000 portraits (including paintings, drawings, sculptures and photographs) of famous men and women from the Middle Ages to the present day. From politicians to poets, and from royalty to pop stars, there is something for everyone to enjoy in this entertaining collection. It starts with the Tudors on the top floor, working down to current celebrities. The gallery houses what is believed to be the only oil portrait of William Shakespeare done from life. Open 10:00–18:00, Saturday–Wednesday, 10:00–21:00, Thursday and Friday. www.npg.org.uk

THE NATIONAL GALLERY

The majority of the capital's modern and British collections of art are found in **Tate Modern** and **Tate Britain**, while the main strengths of the **National Gallery** are in early Renaissance Italian, Dutch, and 17th-century Spanish paintings. Some of the star attractions include the **Leonardo Cartoon** (chalk drawing of the Virgin and Child with St John the Baptist, 1510); the **Baptism of Christ** by Piero della Francesca (a pioneer of early Renaissance perspective, 1450); the **Rokeby Venus** by Diego Velázquez (1649); John Constable's **Haywain** (classic portrayal of the English countryside, 1821) and Hans Holbein's **The Ambassadors** (1533). Monet's **Waterlilies** is among the more modern works.

Opposite top: *Trafalgar Square by day.*
Left: *Trafalgar Square at Christmas. The giant Christmas tree is an annual gift from Norway.*

41

3
The West End

Now in the heart of London, the West End acquired its name in the 19th century, when it was west of the original commercial centre. Then it became a desirable area, with smart shops and hotels establishing themselves among the formal squares and mews terraces. Today the West End is the capital's principal shopping and entertainment district.

London's major theatres and cinemas are concentrated around **Leicester Square** and **Piccadilly Circus**, which form part of **Soho**. Traditionally, Soho has been home to immigrants from Irish, Israeli, Italian, Chinese and even Huguenot descent. The invention of the laundromat forced the Chinese to diversify from traditional laundry businesses in the East End to restaurant ownership. **Chinatown** is now one of the best-known areas in which to enjoy a cheap, tasty meal after the theatre or cinema.

Soho's Bohemian atmosphere has always attracted writers, artists and musicians, and, more recently, media folk. Its dual personality is evident in the existence of porn shops alongside smart clubs and trendy shops. It was largely to distance the up-and-coming area around Mayfair from the relative squalor of Soho that **Regent Street** was laid out in the early 1800s, when over 700 houses and small shops were demolished to make way for Nash's grand design. Today Regent Street and **Bond Street**, are among the capital's classiest shopping streets. Nearby **Savile Row** is famed as the home of bespoke English tailoring, while **Oxford Street** is Europe's busiest shopping street, with 200 million visitors a year.

DON'T MISS

*** Soho: soak up the Bohemian atmosphere.
** Piccadilly: English tea at the **Ritz** or **Fortnum's**.
* Charing Cross Road: browse the bookshops, see the **Photographers' Gallery**.
* Piccadilly Circus: see it by night, followed by a show at a West End theatre.
* Bond Street and **Regent Street:** window-shopping in the exclusive stores.
* Chinatown: exotic supermarkets and great food.

Opposite: *The statue of 'Eros' against a background of neon signs.*

SOHO

One of the city's most colourful areas, Soho buzzes with activity 24 hours a day, particularly by night. Once London's principal red-light district, it has been cleaned up in recent years (although strip joints and sleazy sex clubs still operate) and now offers a vast range of fashionable cafés, brasseries, restaurants, discos, respectable clubs and, of course, cinemas and theatres.

Shaftesbury Avenue is one of the main theatre areas, and also has a few cinemas and clubs. Parallel to Shaftesbury Avenue, **Old Compton Street** is typical of the peculiar mixture which characterizes Soho: sex shops rubbing shoulders with Continental patisseries and cafés, fashion boutiques, gay bars, trendy brasseries and specialized food shops.

There are many interesting little nooks and crannies to be discovered while wandering around the network of streets in this vicinity. **Frith Street** has a plaque on the house where Mozart once stayed, and it was in a room above a restaurant here that John Logie Baird gave the first ever public demonstration of his new invention, the television, in 1926. Ronnie Scott's famous jazz club was founded here in 1959 (*see* p. 24). **Dean Street** boasts a plaque to Karl Marx. Soho's vice rackets are mostly concentrated to the west of **Wardour Street**, where you will also find **Berwick Street market** (a good place to buy fruit).

Charing Cross Road ★

Dividing Soho from Covent Garden to the east, Charing Cross Road boasts several theatres and the highest concentration of bookshops in the city. Other than the rambling expanses of Foyle's and Waterstone's there are

HALF-PRICE THEATRE

On the south side of Leicester Square, the Society of West End Theatres operates **tkts** (a **ticket booth** where you can get seats for the day's performance for as little as half price +£2.50 for most West End shows). It is open 10:00–19:00 Mon–Sat, 12:00–15:00 on Sunday. Tickets are seldom available for sell-out shows, but can sometimes be obtained through official booking agencies such as Keith Prowse, tel: (0870) 906 3838, or Ticketmaster, tel: (0870) 534 4444, if you are prepared to pay hefty booking fees. Buying tickets from touts outside theatres is not advisable.

numerous specialist and second-hand bookshops, particularly in **Cecil Court** below Leicester Square tube station. Nearby is the excellent **Photographers' Gallery** which has interesting (and free) exhibitions. Open 11:00–18:00, Monday–Saturday; 12:00–18:00 on Sunday. www.photonet.org.uk

Leicester Square ★

Adjoining Charing Cross Road, Leicester Square is where all the big movies are premiered and it also has several popular clubs and discos at its fringes. The garden at the centre of the square features a statue of Charlie Chaplin, while a wide variety of street performers make the north side their stage, as do street artists who are happy to create souvenir portraits.

Chinatown ★

To the north of Leicester Square is Chinatown, a small enclave focused around Gerrard Street with its red-and-gold gateways and pagoda-style telephone boxes. Chinese supermarkets and ornament shops co-exist alongside numerous restaurants, open late into the night, where you can find cuisine from many different regions of China. The restaurants here (particularly the smaller ones which look more like cafés) are usually reasonably priced, and full to overflowing on Sundays with Chinese families tucking into their ***dim sum***.

CHINESE NEW YEAR

If you're in the city for the **Chinese New Year** (late Jan or early Feb) head down to **Gerrard Street** to witness one of the noisiest celebrations in the capital, with firecrackers exploding everywhere as colourful papier-mâché lions dance through Chinatown trying to grab the cabbages, decorated with bank notes, which residents hang from their windows. This exuberant event attracts Chinese people, as well as sight-seers, from all over London.

Opposite: *London's famous 'black' cabs (they actually come in 12 official colours – plus advertisements) in Shaftesbury Avenue, where several theatres are located.*
Left: *Chinese New Year is a colourful and joyous celebration when Chinatown comes alive with dragons and parades.*

PICCADILLY AND REGENT STREET
Piccadilly Circus ★

Originally known as Regent Circus and forming part of Nash's grand plan for Regent Street, Piccadilly Circus is one of the main hubs of the West End and a popular tourist spot – although Londoners are more likely to curse the traffic or pedestrian congestion.

Leading south from Piccadilly Circus is Haymarket, home to New Zealand House, once the Carlton Hotel; there is a blue plaque on the wall to commemorate the fact that Vietnamese revolutionary leader Ho Chi Minh (1890–1969) worked here as a waiter in 1913.

Occupying several blocks just off Piccadilly Circus is the London Trocadero complex. The **Trocadero Centre** (main entrance Coventry Street) incorporates a multi-screen cinema and **Funland**: an interactive centre on several floors which includes 10-pin bowling, simulated rides and games. It stays open until midnight or later.

Regent Street ★★

The section of Regent Street that curves between Oxford Circus and Piccadilly Circus is a prime shopping zone, featuring such renowned stores as Hamleys, Aquascutum and Liberty. At the southern end is the **Café Royal**, once frequented by Oscar Wilde and George Bernard Shaw, which retains a faded grandeur.

Behind Hamley's, to the east, is **Carnaby Street**. Once a focal point of the 'Swinging Sixties', it is enjoying a resurgence with stores from some of the world's top brands, including Puma, Ben Sherman, Lee, Van and Diesel. There are also three floors of individual designer shops in

Below: *Piccadilly Circus, with its vast hoardings and 'Eros' statue.*

adjoining **Kingly Court**, where you can sit and relax at a café in a relatively peaceful courtyard.

North of Oxford Circus is Portland Place, home of **Broadcasting House**, the headquarters of the BBC. Opposite here, the Langham is (which is one of the city's oldest posh hotels) was founded in 1865, it's one of the the the Leading Hotels of the World.

Piccadilly ★★

Leading from Piccadilly Circus to Hyde Park Corner, **Piccadilly** is a busy road where you can take afternoon tea at the famous **Ritz Hotel** (if you book weeks ahead) or **Fortnum & Mason**, the epicurean emporium which supplies delicacies to the Royal household, and magnificent picnic hampers for society events.

Behind Fortnum & Mason, there is a small enclave between Piccadilly and the Mall, which has been a fashionable haunt since Henry VIII built St James's Palace in the 1530s, with courtiers and pillars of society disporting themselves ever since in its smart shops and exclusive clubs.

At the heart of this exclusive area is St James's Square, laid out in the 1670s. Some houses here have seen a succession of illustrious residents: No. 10 was home to prime ministers Pitt the Elder, Lord Derby and Gladstone (today it houses the offices of the prestigious Royal Institute of International Affairs). No. 4 was previously the home of Nancy Astor, who became the first female MP to sit in the House of Commons in

Above: *The Tudor-style façade of Liberty, one of London's most exclusive department stores, famous for its fabric designs.*

Below: *The luxurious Fortnum & Mason is the place where you may, among other things, purchase many varieties of tea and other traditional English fare in the ground-floor food hall and sample it in the restaurants.*

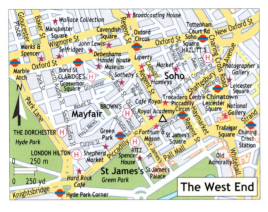

The West End

1919. During World War II, both General Eisenhower and General de Gaulle had headquarters here. At No. 14 is the London Library, a private lending library founded by historian Thomas Carlyle. To the west of St James's Square can be found the auctioneers, Christie's, while just to the south is the unusual Schomberg House, with a 17th-century red brick façade; the painter, Gainsborough, lived here in the last years of his life. Located to the north of St James's Square and running parallel with Piccadilly is Jermyn Street, one of London's most elegant shopping streets. Among the windows that are worth peering into along here are those of Davidoff (cigars, parasols and ornate walking sticks), Turnbull & Asser (shirts), Floris (perfumes), Tricker's (shoemakers to royalty), Paxton & Whitfield (cheesemakers since 1797) and Alfred Dunhill (suppliers of gentlemen's luxury goods).

In St James's Place is **Spencer House**, a splendid 18th-century town house built for the first Earl of Spencer, ancestor of the late Diana, Princess of Wales. In the 1980s Lord Rothschild restored it to its original magnificence, and there are one-hour *not pre-bookable* guided tours 10:30–16:45 on Sundays (closed January and August). Very occasionally the gardens are also open. www.spencerhouse.co.uk

On Piccadilly itself is **St James's Church**, built by Wren in 1684 and said to have been his favourite amongst the many London churches he was responsible for. Although much altered since then (partly due to bomb damage in 1940), it still features an airy, graceful interior and an ornate altar screen carved by the 17th-century master Grinling Gibbons; the organ was moved here from the chapel at the Whitehall Palace in 1691.

Opposite: The Burlington Arcade, built in the 19th century, houses many small and exclusive shops. **Below:** *Floris in Jermyn Street, purveyors of fine fragrances since 1730.*

William Blake and Pitt the Elder were baptised in this church, which today hosts society weddings, lectures, and concerts, as well as ministering to the homeless and hosting markets: antiques on Tuesday, arts and crafts Wednesday–Saturday.

Gentlemen's Clubs ★

Pall Mall and St James's Street are famous for their private clubs, many of which still traditionally exclude women. Most were founded in the early 19th century. The oldest is **White's** (with a membership which includes Prince Charles, top politicians, and military brass), while the **Carlton Club** is favoured by top Tories and the **Reform Club** was traditionally the home of the Liberals.

The Royal Academy ★★

On the north side of Piccadilly, Burlington House is home to the **Royal Academy**. Founded in 1768, it holds many exhibitions annually, including the well-known Summer Exhibition, and is reached via a paved piazza designed specifically for changing exhibitions of sculptures. It is open 10:00–17:30 Sat–Thu; 10:00–21:30 Fri. www.royalacademy.org.uk

Next door is a superb Regency Mall, the Burlington Arcade, with delightful mahogany-fronted shops selling smart shirts, luggage, jewellery and other pricey items.

Turning right at the northern end of the arcade will bring you (on the other side of the street) to **Savile Row**, home to around 30 of Britain's most exclusive tailors.

Shepherd Market ★

Between Mayfair and Piccadilly lies a maze of alleys and passageways, which still retain a village-like atmosphere. Here you will find a number of fashionable restaurants and pubs, from which people overflow onto the pavements in summer.

CHRISTMAS LIGHTS

During the pre-Christmas rush there is no busier place than Oxford Street and the surrounding area, with traffic wardens continually marshalling shoppers to stop them from blocking the roads or falling under the wheels of a bus. Most are probably busy gawking at the famous **Christmas lights** which adorn the streets from November onwards. Oxford Street, Regent Street and Bond Street usually all have **lighting up ceremonies** where celebrities throw the switches, and various jollities are provided, including carol singers, horse-drawn carriages, choirs, musicians, seasonal refreshments and, of course, late-night shopping. Contact VisitLondon (*see* p. 120) for exact dates.

A Day at Selfridges

One of the great landmarks of
Oxford Street is the imposing,
colonnaded façade of
Selfridges, which opened in
1909, just four years after
Harrods in Knightsbridge, and
challenged the latter's domi-
nance by marketing itself as
being 'dedicated to the service
of women'. 'Why not spend a
day at Selfridges?' was the
novel theme promoted by its
owner, Chicago millionaire
Gordon Selfridge. One of its
original Art Deco lifts is now
in the Museum of London
(see p. 74). In 1927, Selfridge
purchased Whiteleys in
Queensway, which had gone
into decline after its founder
William Whiteley (a role
model for Selfridge) had been
murdered. It was Whiteley
who had claimed to supply
everything 'from a pin to an
elephant' – a slogan that was
later associated with Harrods.

Mayfair and Oxford Street
Mayfair ★

Situated to the north of Piccadilly, Mayfair is one of the
most upmarket residential areas in London. It is an
aristocratic enclave where major 18th-century
landowners such as the Berkeleys and Grosvenors built
grand squares (which still bear their names) surrounded
by palatial mansions. Embassies, consulates and swish
hotels (such as Claridge's) now predominate, with top
shopping districts, clubs and casinos (in St James's and
Curzon Street respectively) within convenient reach.

Mayfair is bordered on the west by **Park Lane**, where
luxury hotels such as The Dorchester, Grosvenor House
and The London Hilton enjoy views over Hyde Park.

Bond Street ★★

Cutting right through the heart of Mayfair, Bond Street
(divided into New Bond Street in the north and Old
Bond Street in the south) harbours some of the most
exclusive and expensive shops in London: Chanel,
Asprey, Garrard, Cartier, Versace and Hermès are all
found along here. Bond Street is also noted for its fine
art galleries, and its resident auctioneers, **Sotheby's**.

Handel House Museum ★

In Brook Street (the entrance is in Lancashire Court), is

Handel House Museum, a place
which will appeal to lovers of the
Georgian period even if they are not
fond of the composer himself.
Handel took up residence here in
1723, remaining until his death in
1759. During this time he composed
such masterpieces as *Messiah* (the
original, somewhat messy, manuscript is on display) and *Zadok the
Priest* as well as his music for the
royal fireworks. His home has been
faithfully refurbished, the graceful
Georgian décor forming a perfect

Left: *The Hard Rock Café is one of London's most popular eating places and something of an institution.* **Opposite:** *The Dorchester, Park Lane.*

setting for items covering his life, work and times. There is an extensive programme of special events, including live music. Open 10:00–17:00 Tue–Sat (to 19:30 Thu); 12:00–17:30 Sun and holiday Mon. www.handelhouse.org

Oxford Street ★
One of London's best-known shopping areas, Oxford Street was developed as long ago as the 1780s to cater for the wealthy residents who were at that time moving out of the old city centre into more fashionable areas in the West End. This 2km (1 mile) street is still one of the world's most profitable retailing districts despite numerous recessions and very high rents. There are also a number of good quality department stores such as the flagship store of Marks & Spencer, Selfridges, John Lewis and Debenhams.

The Wallace Collection ★★
In Manchester Square (to the north of Selfridges) is the stunning Wallace Collection. In 1897 Lady Wallace left all the art treasures 'placed on the ground and first floors and in the galleries of Hertford House' to the Nation. These were the accumulated acquisitions of five generations of the Hertford family and almost certainly represent the greatest single bequest of its kind ever made. She added two conditions: the government should build a suitable museum to hold the art treasures; and they should never be mixed with other collections. The collection is, therefore, untainted and the government decided that, rather than build somewhere else, they would acquire Hertford House itself and simply adapt it to provide a suitable setting. The fabulous display includes European furniture, porcelain, sculptures, paintings, including many that are famous, and an impressive armoury – not to mention an excellent courtyard restaurant. Open 10:00–17:00 Mon–Sat; 12:00–17:00 Sun. www.wallacecollection.org

4
Bloomsbury and Covent Garden

A stone's throw from the busy shops of Oxford Street and adjacent Tottenham Court Road (the main centre for hi-fi and computer retailing in London), **Bloomsbury** is, by contrast, a low-key area known for its many pleasant public squares and literary associations. Home to London University and numerous book publishers, the area was also the birthplace of the famous Bloomsbury Group during the inter-war years, an intellectual circle of friends that included Virginia Woolf, DH Lawrence, Bertrand Russell, EM Forster and Lytton Strachey. Today the main attraction in the area is the **British Museum**, a venerable institution which has undergone a major transformation: London's first covered square – and one of its most imaginative public spaces – now forms the heart of this historic museum.

To the south of Bloomsbury, High Holborn leads to the tranquil legal enclaves of the historical buildings of the **Inns of Court**, the main centre of jurisprudence in the city for the last 700 years.

One of the liveliest areas of central London, **Covent Garden** was once the capital's main market for fruit, flowers and vegetables until the wholesale market was moved out to a purpose-built complex south of the Thames near Battersea in 1974. In the last three decades it has been redeveloped and has gradually blossomed as a tourist attraction in its own right, bursting with trendy wine bars and restaurants, smart clothes shops, arts and crafts markets and almost non-stop street entertainment.

DON'T MISS

*** British Museum: utstanding collections. Follow up with a stroll around Bloomsbury's leafy squares and a visit to **Dickens' House Museum.**
*** Somerset House: three stunning collections.
*** Covent Garden: markets, shops and restaurants of this trendy area.
** The Courtauld: Impressionist and Post-Impressionist collections.
** Sir John Soane's Museum: eclectic collections.

Opposite: *Covent Garden's market hall, was London's produce market for over 100 years.*

CHARLES DICKENS

Dickens (1812–70) portrayed London's foggy streets and colourful characters in 16 novels. No stranger to poverty, he became a solicitor's clerk and then a parliamentary reporter, before his first novels were published in instalments in magazines. In later life he toured America giving readings, and died at his desk aged 58.

BLOOMSBURY

This area has a pleasant architectural coherence, and its Georgian squares provide a tranquil respite from the hubbub of city life. On the fringes of Bloomsbury is **Dickens' House Museum** (48 Doughty Street), which gives an interesting insight into the writer's life. Open 10:00–16:30 Mon–Sat; 11:00–16:30 Sun and holidays. www.dickensmuseum.com

In **Brunswick Square** (just off the map) is the **Foundling Museum**, which tells the story of London's first home for abandoned children (open 10:00–18:00 Tue–Sat, 12:00–18:00 Sun). www.foundlingmuseum.org.uk

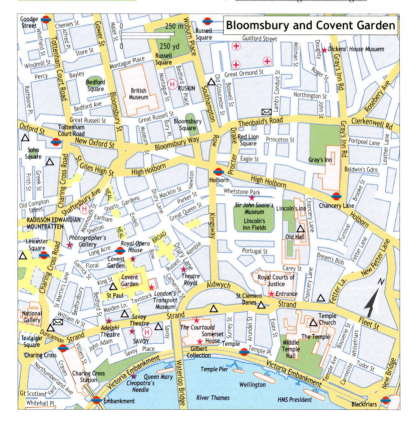

Bloomsbury and Covent Garden

Left: *The British Museum's collections were largely built up in the days of the Empire.*

British Museum ★★★

The British Museum never fails to astound one but, given its size, plan for more than one visit. The extraordinary collections span from prehistoric times to the present day. Founded in the late 18th century, the museum has some seven and a half million exhibits in 88 galleries, requiring a walk of several miles to cover them all. It is one of the country's biggest tourist attractions – and entry is free.

The museum's great strengths are its collections of treasures and artworks from ancient Egypt, Greece and Rome, as well as Asia and the Far East, in addition to superb treasures from Roman and Anglo-Saxon Britain.

It's impossible to digest it all at once, and you might like to opt for one of the audio or guided tours (a fee is payable), which cover many of the highlights. The museum is open 10:00–17:30 Sat–Wed, 10:00–20:30 Thu–Fri. www.thebritishmuseum.ac.uk

Treasures include the Rosetta Stone (dating from 196BC, it unlocked the language of ancient Egypt), mummies of the Pharaohs in the Egyptian Galleries; the human-headed lions and bulls of ancient Assyria; the Elgin Marbles and other Greek masterpieces; the Portland Vase with its exquisitely carved blue and white glass; the Lindow Man (sacrificed during a Druidic ceremony, his well-preserved body was found in peat in 1984), and the Sutton Hoo Anglo-Saxon treasures.

THE GREAT COURT

The British Museum has recently undergone a transformation. The British Library has moved (see p. 83) and the famous **Round Reading Room** (where Marx, Lenin and many other luminaries have studied) is accessible to the general public for the first time – with computer information about exhibits joining the reference books about relevant subjects. The **Great Court** in which it stands has reopened to the public for the first time since 1857: a great covered square at the heart of the museum. For a time the museum's ethnographic collection was set up elsewhere as the **Museum of Mankind**, but the renovations have created sufficient space for the exhibits to be reincorporated into the main museum.

Right: *Covent Garden is always alive with street entertainers and musicians of all kinds.*

Opposite: *A fashionable part of London popular with tourists and Londoners alike, Covent Garden offers a wide choice of restaurants, cafés and wine bars.*

COVENT GARDEN

At the core of Covent Garden is the **piazza** – London's oldest planned square – which was originally designed by Inigo Jones in the 1630s.

It was a very desirable residential area until market traders started moving in, and, later, insalubrious coffee houses, gambling dens and brothels sprang up around the piazza. The central **market hall** was built in the 1830s (the glass roof was added later) and continued to be the country's most important wholesale fruit and vegetable market until it was relocated to Vauxhall in 1974.

Today the market hall, piazza and surrounding streets (particularly in the converted warehouses to the north) are crammed with speciality shops, restaurants, pubs and much more besides. It has become one of London's major tourist attractions.

On the west side of the piazza is **St Paul's Church** – known as the 'Actors' Church' due to its proximity to theatreland – which has numerous memorials to famous actors and actresses. Appropriately enough, the space in front of the church is now the main venue for Covent Garden's **street entertainers**, with jugglers, mime artists, musicians and other buskers.

Facing Bow Street on the east side of the piazza is the **Royal Opera House**, home to the Royal Ballet and Opera. Built in the early 19th century, this grandiose building has recently reopened after major redevelop-

ment and there are tours. Pre-book on
www.royaloperahouse.org

London's Transport Museum **

One of the old market sheds on the east side houses
the museum which traces the history of transport in the
capital from old horse-drawn buses to trams, the underground (the world's oldest, begun in 1863), buses and
much more. There are plenty of interactive exhibits and
such things as old news items and posters can be
viewed. Currently closed for refurbishment, it is due to
re-open in summer 2007. For information, check
www.ltmuseum.co.uk

Theatre Royal, Drury Lane *

This was one of the first theatres to be built in London
after the end of Oliver Cromwell's puritanical rule
(during which theatre-going was banned), and was
completed in 1663. After a fire it was rebuilt in 1812,
and remodelled again in 1921. The staircases and foyer
feature an impressive range of statues and paintings of
famous actors.

An entertaining tour operates twice or
three times daily, led by three actors who
constantly change character and costume.
It is designed to amuse as well as to
educate, including history, ghosts and
backstage areas. Tickets can be obtained
from the box office but it is generally best
to book ahead, tel: (020) 7494 5000.

The theatre is known as Theatre Royal,
Drury Lane, even though the entrance is on
Catherine Street.

STRAND

Connecting Trafalgar Square with Fleet
Street, **Strand** was once on the waterfront.
On the south side of Strand is the **Savoy
Theatre**, adjoining the famous Savoy
Hotel. Opened in 1889, the Savoy is one

of the city's grandest hotels and its forecourt is the only street in the UK where traffic drives on the right. The impressive Art Deco **Thames Foyer** is well worth seeing; you can also enjoy a traditional English tea in these elegant surroundings.

Somerset House ★★★

Built in 1786, on the site of the palace of the Earls of Somerset, this imposing classical building was the first major building in the country to be designed as offices and is now one of the capital's most important show-places for art. Collections open daily 10:00–17:15. www.somerset-house.org.uk

One wing (entered from Strand) now houses the **Courtauld Gallery**, one of the finest collections of paintings in the country, with superb Impressionist and post-Impressionist works, alongside masterpieces from other eras, as well as some sculptures and furniture.

Children enjoy splashing in the 55 jets of water (illuminated at night) that cool the central courtyard in summer and becomes an ice rink in winter. It leads to the wing (with another entrance on the Victoria Embankment, the first London thoroughfare to be lit

by electricity – in 1879) that now houses the **Gilbert Collection**, an awe-inspiring 800-piece collection of decorative arts. There is a spectacular display of large ornamental objects found in the main gallery: mostly featuring a variety of gold, silver and Italian mosaics. There is a side gallery that has a wealth of such small items as snuffboxes and miniatures – even a jewel- encrusted Portuguese crown.

There six **Hermitage Rooms** recreate the atmosphere of the Winter Palace, to provide a setting for changing 6-month-long exhibitions of artefacts on loan from St Petersburg's Hermitage Museum.

The Inns of Court ★

Near Aldwych is the area which has been the focal point of the country's legal system since the 13th century. Here, potential lawyers

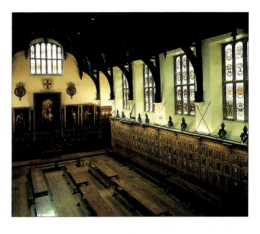

studied, ate and slept at one of the four **Inns of Court** (Gray's Inn, Lincoln's Inn, Middle Temple and Inner Temple), and vestiges of this 'live-in' system of learning still persist today.

Interesting buildings include **Middle Temple Hall**, tel: (020) 7427 4814, with wood-panelled walls that date from the 16th century and portraits of Tudor kings and queens, and **Temple Church**, built in 1185 by the Knights Templar and featuring stone effigies of Crusaders and lovely stained glass. Both are open to the public when not in use for functions. The latter has become a tourist magnet since publication of *The Da Vinci Code* and the Master of the Temples gives regular talks about it, usually late morning/early afternoon, but very variable, tel: (020) 7353 3470 for schedules.

Sir John Soane's Museum ★★

On the north side of Lincoln's Inn Fields, this museum is one of London's best kept secrets. Based on the personal accumulation of art works and antiques of architect Sir John Soane, this unusual collection includes works by Hogarth, Reynolds, Turner and Canaletto, and many of his architectural drawings. In the basement of this intriguing house is the Egyptian sarcophagus of Seti I. Open 10:00–17:00, Tue–Sat. www.soane.org

Above: *Middle Temple Hall has a splendid Elizabethan hammerbeam roof and was the setting for the first performance of William Shakespeare's Twelfth Night in 1602.*
Opposite: *A snuffbox of Frederick the Great, part of the Gilbert Collection.*

ROYAL COURTS OF JUSTICE

This imposing building on Strand is open to visitors 09:00–16:30, Monday–Friday, October–July. There is a display of legal robes and, more importantly, you can visit one of the 81 courts to see British justice in action.

5
West and
Southwest London

Separated from Notting Hill and Bayswater by the green expanse of Hyde Park, the Royal Borough of **Kensington** still has an air of exclusivity about it, although it is no longer the aristocratic suburb it was over 100 years ago. **Kensington Palace**, a royal residence, adjoins **Kensington Gardens** and **Hyde Park**, which together form London's largest park. To the south, **Knightsbridge** is a smart residential area – the famous **Harrods** store its main attraction.

Several of London's top museums are located in **South Kensington** ('South Ken' to Londoners), with the **Victoria and Albert**, **Natural History** and **Science museums** next door to each other. These are the legacy of the 1851 **Great Exhibition of the Works of Industry of All Nations**, keenly promoted by Prince Albert, Queen Victoria's consort. It featured a unique wrought-iron and glass 'Crystal Palace' as its centrepiece, filled with exhibits from around the world. On the southern side of Hyde Park, the Crystal Palace drew over six million visitors and the Exhibition's profits were used to buy 35ha (87 acres) of land nearby to create a 'Museumland' that would promote the arts and sciences. This led to the creation of South Kensington's museums. The palace was torn down and reconstructed in southeast London, where it burned down in 1936.

Neighbouring **Chelsea** features many tranquil mews houses and prime residential streets, such as Cheyne Walk on the banks of the Thames. However, its best-known thoroughfare is **King's Road**, birthplace of the 'Swinging Sixties'.

Opposite: *The Natural History Museum.*

WHITELEYS

In 1885, William Whiteley opened the country's first real department store and, in 1896, Queen Victoria granted it a Royal Warrant. It went into decline after WWII, but reopened in 1989, having been restored to its Edwardian glory. It pioneered mail order – and Hitler planned to use it as his British HQ. Nowadays the lower floors are filled with shops, while the upper floors are for entertainment, with an eight-screen cinema, restaurants varying from Chinese to Tex-Mex and changing art exhibitions. The complex is open 08:30––24:00 daily. Shops open 10:00–20:00 or 22:00 Mon–Sat, 12:00–18:00 Sun.

NOTTING HILL CARNIVAL

From Sat through to Mon on the Aug Bank Holiday weekend every year, the Notting Hill area heaves with people celebrating the famous **Carnival** – ear-splitting reggae, Caribbean soca, hip-hop and other music booms out from dozens of sound systems set up in the streets. The main events are the costume parades on Sun and Mon, and a steel band contest on Sat, with massive, colourful floats and extraordinarily ornate costumes. There are also several stages for live music, and stalls everywhere selling Red Stripe, Jamaican patties and other exotica.

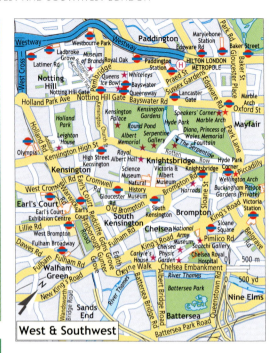

West & Southwest

NOTTING HILL AND BAYSWATER

To the north and northwest of Hyde Park respectively, both Bayswater and Notting Hill are characterized by the contrast of smart terraces and sweeping crescents alongside rather down-at-heel areas, with similarly cosmopolitan populations – in the case of Bayswater, largely Arabic and Chinese communities, and in Notting Hill mostly Afro-Caribbean.

Queensway ★

With Hyde Park at its southern end, Queensway is a hive of activity, offering lots of eateries. At No. 17 is **Queens Ice Bowl**, home to London's only permanent **ice-skating rink** and **ten-pin bowling** alleys. Open daily 10:00–23:30 for bowling; daily 10:00–18:45 for skating, with evening sessions 20:00–22:45 Mon–Thu and 19:30–22:45 Fri–Sun. www.queensicebowl.com

Notting Hill ★

Notting Hill was one of the first areas to receive a post-war influx of immigrants from the Caribbean and saw the country's first race riots in 1958, when black-white competition for jobs and housing turned to violence. Partly to re-assert their Afro-Caribbean identity, the community organized the first **Notting Hill Carnival** in the early 1960s. Held every August Bank Holiday, it is now Europe's biggest street festival – the largest carnival in the world after Rio.

Portobello Road market, at its best Saturday, features everything from antiques to food, in an environment bursting with atmosphere.

In nearby Colville Mews is the nostalgic **Museum of Brands, Packaging and Advertising**, where a time tunnel of consumer goods leads from Victorian times to the present. Open 10:00–18:00 Tue–Sat, 11:00–16:00 Sun and holiday Mon. www.museumofbrands.com

HYDE PARK

London's largest park, Hyde Park was originally a hunting ground for Henry VIII, and was first opened to the public during the reign of James I. Together with adjoining Kensington Gardens it provides a massive open space (covering 250ha/618 acres) in the heart of the city, a haven for dog-walkers, joggers, horseriders and skateboarders.

At the centre of the park is the **Serpentine**, a long, artificial lake that is popular for rowing and swimming daily, open 10:00–18:00 June–Sept. On the south side of the lake, the **Serpentine Gallery** holds interesting exhibitions of contemporary art. Open daily 10:00–18:00. www.serpentinegallery.org

Below: *Portobello Road is one of London's best-known antique markets.*

Right: *Horse riding is popular in Hyde Park along Rotten Row (the name is a corruption of route du roi).*
Opposite: *The food hall at Harrods, in Knightsbridge, London's most famous department store, where the emphasis is on quality.*

Below: *Speaker's Corner at Marble Arch, where anyone who wishes may address the crowds.*

Just east of here is the **Diana, Princess of Wales Memorial Fountain**. This controversial £3.6m monument, an oval ring built from Cornish granite and filled with water, was designed by the American landscape architect Kathryn Gustafson. Open 10:00 all year – closing times vary.

In Hyde Park's northeastern corner is **Marble Arch**, which was moved here in 1851 from outside Buckingham Palace. Marble Arch stands on what is essentially one of two traffic islands split by a bus lane at the west end of Oxford Street, but both have been greened up to form an extension to Hyde Park. Across from Marble Arch is **Speaker's Corner**, which has been a rallying point for political dissent since the 1850s, and is now best known for the soap-box orators who regularly entertain the crowds here (particularly on Sunday mornings).

Park Lane runs down the east side of the park to **Hyde Park Corner**, where **Wellington Arch**, topped by Europe's largest bronze sculpture (the Angel of Peace descending on the Chariot of War), offers changing exhibitions and good views. Open 10:00–16:30 Wed–Sun. On the northwest side of Hyde Park Corner is

Apsley House, a remarkable mansion which was, once upon a time, the home of the Duke of Wellington (during his lifetime the house was referred to as Number One, London). Built by Robert Adam between 1771 and 1778, the house was occupied by the 'Iron Duke' when he was at the height of his career as the most powerful commander in Europe, and the lavish interior fittings, furnishings and paintings (which include works by Rubens, Velázquez, Goya and Correggio) reflect his stature. Open 10:00–17:00 (summer), 10:00–16:00 (winter) Tue–Sun.

From Hyde Park Corner running along the south of the park is **Rotten Row**, a fashionable bridlepath where the Household Cavalry exercise every morning from their nearby barracks. Past here is the **Albert Memorial**, opposite the **Royal Albert Hall** on Kensington Gore (*see* p. 67).

KNIGHTSBRIDGE

Knightsbridge and neighbouring Belgravia boast some of the priciest real estate in the capital, with numerous embassies and exclusive hotels scattered throughout their secluded squares. The main attraction for visitors, however, is **Harrods** – a store which actually imposes a dress code: no shorts, ripped jeans or vest tops are allowed – on Brompton Road. More than 30,000 people pass through its doors every day to shop in one of 300 departments spread over seven floors; its post-Christmas sale attracts 10 times that many people. If your time is limited, don't miss the Art Deco food halls on the ground floor. Open 10:00–20:00, Mon–Sat. Nearby **Harvey Nichols** (which is known as 'Harvey Nicks' to its regular customers) is another top department store much favoured by the Sloane set. Open 10:00–20:00 Mon–Sat, 12:00–18:00 Sun.

HARRODS

This internationally famous store, which was originally a tea-dealer's shop in the City, moved into Knightsbridge in 1849 and began selling perfumes, medicines and stationery, as well as groceries. By 1880 it employed nearly 100 assistants, and in 1898 installed London's first escalator – with a member of staff standing at the top ready to revive customers with brandy and smelling salts. The present building, which is illuminated at night, dates from 1905. Today, Harrods employs over 3000 staff and is owned by the Egyptian Al Fayed brothers.

Opposite top:
*Model boating is popular
on the Round Pond in
Kensington Gardens.*
Below: *Kensington Palace
houses royal apartments
but a part of it is also
open to the public.*

KENSINGTON
Kensington Gardens ★★

The westerly extension of Hyde Park, Kensington
Gardens were once the private grounds of
Kensington Palace. The Gardens became a public
park in 1841, and now merge seamlessly with Hyde
Park itself. The delightful gardens feature several
ornamental fountains and statues – the latter including Jacob Epstein's *Rima* as well as the famous statue
of JM Barrie's fictional *Peter Pan* by George
Frampton (dating from 1912) which has sculpted
squirrels, mice, rabbits, birds and fairies cavorting at
its base. The Round Pond, just near Kensington
Palace, is very popular with children (and indeed
adults) piloting model boats. The splendid play-
ground in the park is a memorial to Diana, Princess
of Wales, who lived in Kensington Palace until her
tragic death in 1997.

Kensington Palace ★★

Kensington Palace, at the western end of Kensington
Gardens, was originally a modest country mansion
before being transformed by William of Orange in
1689, and parts of it are still a royal residence. The
self-guided audio tour explains the garments in the
extensive collection of **royal costumes** and leads you
through the State Apartments. The main highlights are
the trompe l'oeil galleries above the King's Staircase;

the King's Gallery (with works
by Rubens and Van Dyck);
Queen Victoria's Bedroom,
where she woke one morning
in June 1837 to find her uncle
had died and she was Queen.
Open daily, 10:00–17:00
Mar–Oct; 10:00–16:00 Nov–
Feb. Take tea in the superb
(and expensive) **Orangery**,
originally built for Queen
Anne. www.hrp.org.uk

AROUND KENSINGTON

Kensington High Street has a range of shops from large stores to small boutiques, and branches of major chains such as **Gap**. Running north from St Mary Abbots church is **Kensington Church Street** which specializes in antiques. You'll find several good French patisseries and bakeries near the **Institut Français** in South Kensington.

Holland Park ★★

This charming park covers just 22ha (54 acres) but within it there are woodland areas (at their best in May, when the azaleas and rhododendrons are in bloom), rose gardens, formal flower gardens, an iris garden and a Japanese garden (created for the 1991 London Festival of Japan). The park, open from 7:30 until dusk throughout the year, was once the private garden of 17th-century Holland House, largely destroyed by Nazi bombing in World War II. The remains of the house now contain a youth hostel and restaurant (in the former orangery), whilst the terrace is used as an open-air theatre during summer.

In Holland Park Road is **Leighton House**, a fascinating 19th-century building that was once the home of Lord Leighton, a leading artist and collector of his time. The extraordinary Arab Hall, designed to show off his collection of Syrian tiles, is a highlight and much of his own work can be seen throughout the building, along with paintings by such contemporaries as Millais. Open 11:00–17:30, Wed–Mon, including the public holidays. www.leightonhouse.co.uk

Below: *Holland Park, although not large, includes impressive gardens and blooms.*

Above: *The Albert Memorial.*
Opposite: *Modelled on a Roman amphitheatre, the Royal Albert Hall is one of the capital's largest concert halls.*

SOUTH KENSINGTON

Situated between Knightsbridge and Kensington is South Kensington, an area renowned for its high Victorian architecture and three of the world's best museums.

Victoria and Albert Museum ★★★

Housing the world's largest collection of decorative art and design pieces, the huge Victoria and Albert Museum usually requires more than just one visit. Founded with proceeds from the Great Exhibition of 1851, it is generally known simply as the V&A. The museum spans over two millennia, housing an extraordinary range of displays which include one of the world's most comprehensive jewellery collections, Europe's largest dress collection, British artefacts of every type, and the largest exhibition of Indian art outside India. Open 10:00–17:45 Thu–Tue, 10:00–22:00 Wed and last Fri of the month. www.vam.ac.uk

Natural History Museum ★★★

The Romanesque-style exterior of the Natural History Museum on Exhibition Road may look forbidding, but the interior houses many interesting interactive exhibits and imaginative displays on the natural world – some of these are geared specifically to children, although they are of course also an important resource for students and zoologists.

On entering the main building you are immediately confronted with a massive, 26m (83ft) skeleton of a *Diplodocus*, signalling one of the museum's major attractions for the younger generation, with their enduring fascination with dinosaurs. This is fully exploited in the superb **Dinosaur Gallery**. Other popular displays are **Creepy Crawlies** (with enlarged models of all sorts of insects, spiders and crustaceans) and **Ecology** (where all forms of life are found). Open 10:00–17:30, Mon–Sat; 11:00–17:30, Sun. www.nhm.ac.uk

Science Museum ★★★

Another colossus – best digested in manageable chunks – the Science Museum extends over seven floors. The original museum covered everything from transport to space travel and chemistry to telecommunications, with plenty of hands-on exhibits. The **Wellcome Wing** is a hi-tech extension crammed with interactive items, while the basement is packed with goodies for kids of all ages. Exhibits are constantly updated to keep pace with the latest developments in technology. There are also (not free) a state-of-the-art IMAX cinema and virtual reality simulators. Open daily 10:00–18:00.
www.sciencemuseum.org.uk

Royal Albert Hall and Albert Memorial ★

The vast **Royal Albert Hall** was completed in 1871 and has witnessed everything from rock concerts and religious revival meetings to tennis matches. Its most high-profile performances are the annual Promenade Concerts.

Opposite the Royal Albert Hall, in Kensington Gardens, is the **Albert Memorial**, completed in 1876. It has a spire inlaid with semi-precious stones and a frieze depicting 169 life-size figures of scientists, painters, musicians, poets and architects. The memorial has recently been restored, returning it to its original Victorian Gothic splendour, adorned with gilded angels and bright mosaics. The seated figure of Prince Albert, holding a catalogue of the Great Exhibition, has been coated with two layers of gold leaf, as he was originally. Every figure has significance and there are guided 45-minute tours (which go inside the railings for close inspection) at 14:00 and 15:00 on the first Sunday of summer months. Tel: (020) 7495 5504.

SWINGING CHELSEA

The first Continental-style coffee bar opened on the corner of Markham Street in the early 1960s, and the first boutique shortly thereafter; from these small beginnings King's Road grew into the focal point of the 'Swinging Sixties', a busy scene centred on fashion, music, and youth culture where you might well have bumped into the likes of Mick Jagger, David Bailey, Michael Caine, Jane Birkin, Mary Quant or George Best.

Below: *A typical street in Chelsea. One of London's smarter areas, it boasts many elegant townhouses.*

CHELSEA

A short walk from either Knightsbridge or South Kensington, Chelsea has always been a mecca for dedicated followers of fashion. Chelsea is still one of *the* places to see and be seen, to shop – for everything from cult clubwear to classic brand-name clothes – and to spot famous rock stars, royalty or supermodels. It rose to fame in the 1960s with the arrival of 'Swinging London', when the 'Chelsea set' dictated fashion trends (the miniskirt being one of them) which the world followed. The pattern was repeated in the late 1970s, with the creation of punk. Chelsea still keeps abreast of the times, and many of London's sassiest young designers are based here today.

Running through the heart of Chelsea is **King's Road**, with **Sloane Square** at one end, and World's End at the other, chock-a-block with trendy shoe shops, indoor antique markets, fashion boutiques, bars and coffee shops. Although perhaps not as star-studded now as it once was,

it is still a fun place to be – particularly on Saturday afternoons, when it is at its busiest. King's Road was initially a farmers' track which passed through Chelsea's market gardens. It later became a private royal thoroughfare used by King Charles II as a way of avoiding carriage congestion when visiting his mistress, Nell Gwynne, in Fulham. It was most likely a short cut to Hampton Court.

Chelsea is also famous for its Royal Hospital, the grounds of which house the annual **Chelsea Flower Show**.

The **National Army Museum**, also on Royal Hospital Road, traces the history of the British Army from Tudor times to the present, including personal reminiscences and overseas campaigns. Open daily 10:00–17:30.
www.national-army-museum.ac.uk

Left: *Chelsea Pensioners, in their characteristic scarlet uniforms and medals, are part of the Chelsea landscape.*

Chelsea Embankment ★

One of the most famous addresses in Chelsea is **Cheyne Walk**, whose Georgian and Queen Anne houses looked right over the Thames until the building of the Embankment in 1874. Among the many celebrities who have lived here are novelists Henry James (No. 21) and George Eliot (No. 4); pre-Raphaelite painter Dante Gabriel Rossetti (No. 16); artists Whistler (No. 93) and Turner (No. 118) and, more recently, pop stars Mick Jagger (No. 48) and Keith Richard (No. 3). Just around the corner at 24 Cheyne Row is **Carlyle's House** where historian Thomas Carlyle's personal effects have been kept as they were when he died in 1881. Open 14:00–17:00 Wed–Fri, 11:00–17:00 Sat, Sun and holiday Mon, Easter–Oct. www.carlyleshouse.co.uk

Chelsea Physic Garden ★★

One of the great delights of Chelsea is this little-known garden in Royal Hospital Road. It marks the beginning of Cheyne Walk and is the second oldest botanical garden in England after Oxford's. It was founded by the Society of Apothecaries in 1673 and used to teach physicians the medicinal uses of plants and herbs from all over the world. The garden contains over 5000 plants, including the UK's largest outdoor olive tree. At the entrance, maps are available with a list of the most interesting flowers and shrubs. Open 12:00–17:00 Wed, 12:00–18:00 Sun, Apr–Oct. www.chelseaphysicgarden.co.uk

EARLS COURT

Southwest of Kensington is Earls Court, a lively area where it's possible to find reasonable-cost accomodation and cheap eating places. It is also home to a vast hall where exhibitions of all types are staged.

THOMAS MORE

The 16th-century scholar and statesman **Thomas More**, martyred by Henry VIII in 1535, was a long-term resident of Chelsea. He is commemorated by a statue on the Chelsea Embankment, at the end of Cheyne Walk.

SAATCHI GALLERY

After a disastrous fire, the Saatchi Gallery re-located temporarily to County Hall but has now found a new home in Chelsea. It will re-open in 2007 (in the Duke of York's Building, off King's Road) and continue to exhibit the often controversial work of contemporary artists. You can check its currant location on www.saatchi-gallery.co.uk

6. The City, the East End and Docklands

The City of London, as it is known, is London's commercial and financial heartland. The area, steeped in history, includes many famous sights and institutions, including the Bank of England, the Royal Exchange, the Stock Exchange, the Monument to the Great Fire of London, the Central Criminal Court at the Old Bailey and the Mansion House, which is the residence of the Lord Mayor of London (*see* p. 16).

The most enduring legacy from medieval times is the fascinating **Tower of London**, begun by William the Conqueror and completed in the 14th century. Along with Christopher Wren's masterpiece – **St Paul's Cathedral** – the Tower is not to be missed.

In the 1980s, the City underwent a building boom which resulted in the **Broadgate Centre** and the controversial **Lloyd's of London** building (*see* p. 75) followed 20 years later by the **Swiss Re Tower**, completed in 2004.

The East End is traditionally a working class district where the main attractions are the excellent markets.

To the east of the City is the area known as **Docklands**, best viewed from a pleasure boat coursing up the Thames. Not the most obvious of tourist attractions within the capital, it is nevertheless a fascinating area – not least because it is the largest urban regeneration project in the world, a status symbolized by the domineering presence of Cesar Pelli's 245m (803ft) high **Canary Wharf Tower**, one of the tallest in Europe, but current planning applications include higher buildings and the whole skyline is constantly changing.

DON'T MISS

*** Tower of London: an interesting guided tour, led by Beefeaters – and the **Crown Jewels**.
*** Tower Bridge: views from this walkway as well as the Golden Gallery at the top of **St Paul's Cathedral**.
** Museum of London: charts the fascinating history of London.
** Museum in Docklands: learn about the dramatic history of the area.
* Markets: the bustling East End at weekends.

Opposite: *Night-time illuminations reveal the grand façade of St Paul's.*

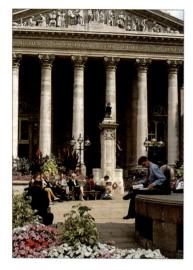

Above: *The Royal Exchange. The City is a major centre for international business.*

THE CITY

The City of London, often called the 'Square Mile' is roughly the area that was originally covered by Roman Londinium. It was almost destroyed in the Great Fire of 1666 and suffered in the Blitz of 1940, but there is still plenty of interest. Although full of modern buildings, the City's streets and alleys still largely follow the Medieval layout.

St Paul's Cathedral ***

St Paul's presents a magnificent façade, with its two baroque towers capped by a 111m (364ft) dome (second in size only to St Peter's in Rome). Wren's airy design is immediately apparent on entering (open 08:30–16:00 Mon–Sat), with the impressive dome featuring a series of trompe l'oeil frescos on the life of St Paul. In the north aisle of the nave is a bronze and marble monument to the Duke of Wellington. In the North Transept is Holman Hunt's *The Light of the World*.

The enormous crypt is reached via the South Transept, and contains some 350 memorials and over 100 tombs. Recent additions include a memorial to British troops who died in the Falklands, but pride of place goes to the tombs of Wellington and Nelson. Artists (such as Turner and Reynolds) are buried here, as are scientist Alexander Fleming, and Wren himself, whose epitaph reads: '*reader, if you seek his monument, look around you*'. The first of the galleries under the dome is the Whispering Gallery; the second is the Stone Gallery, and the third is the Golden Gallery (627 steps up) with fabulous views over the City. ww.stpauls.co.uk South of St Paul's, the innovative **Millennium Bridge** provides great river views and a direct pedestrian link to Tate Modern.

Fleet Street ★

Fleet Street first became a haunt for scribes in the 15th century. In 1702 Britain's first daily newspaper, the *Daily Courant*, was published here, and from the 19th century onwards nearly every major paper had printing presses in the vicinity.

Just off the south side of Fleet Street is **St Bride's**, known as the 'journalists' church', which was designed by Wren. The crypt contains a small museum of Fleet Street history. Open 09:00–16:30 Mon–Fri and some weekends. www.stbrides.com. In Gough Square (a little to the north of Fleet Street) is **Dr Johnson's House**, which was home to the great writer and lexicographer from 1747–59. The house contains some unusual memorabilia as well as etchings and portraits of Dr Johnson and his biographer, Boswell. Open Mon–Sat 11:00–17:00 Oct–Apr; 11:00–17:30 May–Sep; closed holiday Mon. www.drjohnsonshouse.org

The Barbican Complex ★

This large, concrete-clad residential complex was built in the 1970s. At the heart of it is the **Barbican Arts Centre** (a confusing warren covering 12 levels, three of them underground), which is home to the London Symphony Orchestra, the Guildhall School of Music and Drama, cinemas and a concert hall. For details and times of performances, tel: (0845) 121 6828. www.barbican.org.uk

Below: *The ceiling of St Paul's Cathedral.*

Museum of London ★★

Adjacent to the Barbican Complex, the Museum
of London charts the development of the capital
from prehistoric times up to the present, with
appropriate sound effects and interactive screens.

The history of London begins with the
'London Before London' Gallery and offering a
most impressive account of the Roman era in its
Roman Gallery, where objects include the latest
archaeological finds from around the City,
mosaics, sculptures, recreations of shops and
rooms in villas, as well as models of public
baths, the waterfront and the old fort. On the
same floor the tale continues in chronological
order through medieval times to the Great Fire of
London in 1666. Highlights include the **Cheapside
Hoard** (spectacular jewellery spanning several centuries), a model of the **Rose** theatre and the **Great Fire
Experience** (a small diorama with a tape of diarist
Samuel Pepys's first-hand account).

Downstairs (passing the entrance to a peaceful **Nursery
Garden**) the display begins with the Stuart period and continues to the 20th century. Exhibits here include costumes
and music from various periods, a recreated **Victorian
Street**, prison cells and a whipping frame, vehicles from an
early cab to the gilded **Lord Mayor's Coach**, obsolete
machines and all sorts of bric-a-brac. Interactive screens
are scattered through the museum. Open 10:00–17:30
Mon–Sat; 12:00–17:30 Sun. www.museumoflondon.org.uk

Guildhall ★

In the heart of the City, the Guildhall has been
London's administrative centre for over 800 years and
still houses the offices of the Corporation of London.
The Great Hall (10:00–16:30 weekdays) features coats
of arms and banners from the City's guilds and livery
companies. The **Guildhall Art Gallery** (open
10:00–16:30 Mon–Sat; 12:00–15:30 Sun) houses some
250 of the corporation's paintings from the 17th to
20th centuries. www.guildhall-art-gallery.org.uk

THE CITY

75

The Monument ★

The Monument, Monument Street, is a 61m-high column, designed by Christopher Wren, which commemorates the Great Fire of London in 1666 (*see p. 74*) – the fit can climb 311 steps for spectacular views (and receive a certificate for the achievement). Open daily 09:00–17:00, but currently closed for restoration.

The Tower of London ★★★

One of the capital's most popular attractions, the Tower of London is a well-preserved medieval fortress which in its heyday housed around 1500 people. Over the last 900 years it has been a royal palace, a prison, an execution site, an armoury, and is today a repository for the Crown Jewels. Open 09:00–17:00 Tue–Sat, 10:00–17:00 Sun–Mon in summer; 09:00–16:00 Tue–Sat, 10:00–16:00 Sun–Mon in winter. The Yeoman Warders (Beefeaters) conduct frequent (free) tours which are both informative and amusing, so highly recommended – you can join and leave the groups at will, so make your own pace. www.tower-of-london.org.uk or www.hrp.org.uk

DICK WHITTINGTON

The pantomime character of Dick Whittington, with his knapsack and cat, was based on the life of Richard Whittington, a wealthy merchant who first became Mayor of London in 1397. He was a great public benefactor and when he died, childless, in 1423, his fortune was bequeathed to civic works. By the 1500s his rags-to-riches story had become a legend, with Whittington (and his cat) poised to leave the city when he hears the Bow bells ring out 'turn again, Whittington, thrice Lord Mayor of London'. In fact, he was Mayor four times: a stone on Highgate Hill commemorates the spot where he is supposed to have heard the bells. There is also a stained glass window in his honour in St Michael Paternoster Royal in Skinner's Lane in the City.

Opposite: *Lloyd's of London is an architectural landmark in the heart of the City.*
Left: *The Tower of London was used to hold prisoners from medieval times.*

Above: *Beefeaters have been guarding the Tower since Henry VIII's time.*
Right: *The Queen's House in the Tower of London.*
Opposite: *Tower Bridge still opens for tall ships.*

The centre of the complex is the **White Tower**, which dates back to the time of William the Conqueror. Inside are displays of arms and armour, including some used by Henry VIII. There is also an exhibition of torture instruments, along with an axe and block used for executions at the Tower. On the first floor is the beautiful 11th century **St John's Chapel**, the oldest church in London.

In the northeastern corner is the **Martin Tower**, which houses a permanent exhibition, Crowns and Diamonds, which includes some rare 18th- and 19th-century crown frames used at coronations.

Many prisoners arrived at the Tower by boat, entering via the **Traitor's Gate** before being incarcerated in one of the many fortified towers surrounding Tower Green, in the middle of the complex. Situated directly behind the Traitor's Gate is the **Bloody Tower**, where 12-year-old Edward V and his 10-year-old brother, the Duke of York, were (allegedly) murdered on the orders of Richard III. On the west side of the Bloody Tower is the **Queen's House** (now the home of the Tower's Governor and closed to the public) which was built by Henry VIII and used as a prison for Katherine Howard, Anne Boleyn and Lady Jane Grey; the last inmate was Hitler's Deputy, Rudolph Hess.

Nearby is **Tower Green**, the site of several executions, and the spot is marked by a plaque listing the names of the

victims. These include two of Henry VIII's wives, Anne Boleyn and Katharine Howard, Lady Jane Grey, the nine day queen, and the Earl of Essex, Elizabeth I's favourite. Behind is the church of **St Peter ad Vincula**, where they were all buried, without any memorial.

On the northern side of the compound the **Crown Jewels** are on display; a moving walkway carries you past them. The sparkling exhibits include the Crown of State (bedecked with thousands of jewels including a 317-carat diamond), the Koh-i-Noor diamond, sceptres, orbs and other glittering regal paraphernalia.

Tower Bridge ★★

Tower Bridge is a marvel of Victorian engineering (it took eight years to build) and was first opened to traffic on 30 June 1894. It was designed so that tall sailing ships could reach the Port of London – ships still have precedence over road traffic, although compared to the early years (when it was raised over 6000 times a year) it is seldom raised: fewer than 1000 times a year; tel: (020) 7940 3984 for schedule. The 1000 ton bascules were originally raised using pure hydraulic power, but electricity is used today.

The bridge was built in the Gothic style to blend in with the Tower of London, but beneath its stonework exterior is a steel frame which you can see when you get inside. The **Tower Bridge Exhibition** (open daily 10:00–17:30 in summer, 09:30–17:00 in winter) provides a lift up the north tower so that you can cross the Thames by the top walkway – with terrific views – to descend the south tower, from where you can visit the **Engine Room**. There are informative videos en route. www.towerbridge.org.uk

Docklands

— Docklands Light Railway

THE EAST END AND DOCKLANDS

The East End has a colourful past and has been a focal point for immigrants and refugees, from the Huguenots onwards. Recently, the East End has acquired a new lease of life as a focus for contemporary art, with hundreds of artists living and working in the area (including the *enfant terrible* of the contemporary art world, Damien Hirst). Several influential galleries are located here, including the famed Whitechapel Art Gallery.

Street Markets ★

Of all the markets in this area, the oldest and best-known is **Petticoat Lane** (*see* p. 119), which is mainly clothing. Just to the north is the **Spitalfields market**, once the centre of the fruit and vegetable trade (now mostly crafts). East of here and at the heart of London's Bengali community, **Brick Lane** market (bric-a-brac and clothes) tempts passers-by with the aroma of curry wafting out from behind the stalls. **Columbia Road** is an enjoyable street filled with plant and flower stalls. All these markets are best on the weekends. The nearest tube stations are Liverpool Street and Aldgate East.

Whitechapel Art Gallery ★

One of London's top contemporary art galleries is in the heart of the East End: the Whitechapel Art Gallery was founded by a Victorian philanthropist and today often stages unusual exhibitions of avant-garde art from around the world. Open 11:00–18:00 Tue–Sun (until 21:00 Thu). www.whitechapel.org

Bethnal Green Museum of Childhood ★

The museum, in Cambridge Heath Road, houses a superb collection of toys and games past and present, including teddy bears, doll's houses and puppets. Open 10:00–17:30 daily, inc. bank holidays.
www.museumofchildhood.org.uk

Docklands ★

Best known for its hotchpotch of architectural styles, Docklands offers charming riverside pubs, restored warehouses, sailing ships, and even the urban **Mudchute Farm**. Docklands is a catch-all term for a vast area extending east from London Bridge along the Thames, covering 22km² (8½ sq miles), bigger than the City of London and West End combined, with over 88km (55 miles) of waterfront. **St Katharine's Dock**, east of the Tower, has a marina, old swing bridges and an 18th-century pub, the **Dickens' Inn**. Further east, Limehouse, where the city's first Chinese community settled, is home to Hawksmoor's **St Anne's Church**, Commercial Road, distinguished by its church clock: the highest in the City. The Isle of Dogs is now the commercial hub of Docklands and West India Docks is home to the massive **Canary Wharf** development. You can get a really good view of the development from a river boat but, to get into the heart of Docklands, take the **Docklands Light Railway** (DLR) from Bank or Tower Gateway station to Canary Wharf.

Below: *St Katharine's Dock was one of the first of the old docks to undergo redevelopment.*

7
North London

The dividing line between Central and North London is formed by the busy Marylebone and Euston Roads. Once known as New Road, this was the city's first bypass, built in 1756 to allow cattle to be herded from west of the city to Smithfield market without clogging up Oxford Street. The main attraction on Marylebone Road is **Madame Tussauds** waxworks museum, consistently one of London's most popular sights, now with the added attraction of an Aardman Animations star show.

North of Marylebone Road is **Regent's Park**, laid out in the early 1800s and home to **London Zoo** since 1834. Winding its way around the park's northern edge and passing through the zoo itself is the **Regent's Canal**, built to link the Grand Junction Canal at Paddington (which led in turn to the thriving industrial north) with the docks.

Beyond Regent's Park is elegant **Hampstead**, whose village-like atmosphere has appealed to artists, writers and celebrities of all kinds for many years. Spreading in a great swathe northwards from Hampstead is **Hampstead Heath**, one of the largest open spaces in the capital encompassing a range of landscapes including untamed woodland, ponds and lakes, meadows and fields. It is a popular venue for all sorts of activities, including open-air concerts at the historic **Kenwood House**.

To the east of Hampstead lies **Camden Town**, one of the capital's favourite weekend venues, with a vast network of market stalls sprawling around the Regent's Canal at Camden Lock. Both **Islington** and **Clerkenwell**, further east, are well worth a visit.

DON'T MISS

*** Regent's Park: a walk along the canalside combined with a visit to **London Zoo**, rowing on the lake or a visit to the **Open Air Theatre**.
** Hampstead: explore the village and the wild spaces of **Hampstead Heath**.
** Camden: catch up on the latest fashions in the busy markets here.
** Madame Tussauds: incredible waxworks displays.
* Camden Passage: browse through the antique stalls and shops.

Opposite: *One of London's many famous graveyards, Highgate Cemetery features an array of unusual statuary.*

Above: *Queen Elizabeth I, one of hundreds of wax dummies at the renowned Madame Tussauds.*

Below: *Even Aardman's creations flock to Madame Tussauds!*

MARYLEBONE
Madame Tussauds ★★

One of the most popular tourist attractions in the capital, this famous waxworks museum attracts two to three million visitors annually and you should expect to queue a long time for tickets. It is possible to avoid the worst queue by purchasing tickets in advance: sources include tel: (0870) 400 3000, www.madame-tussauds.com and tourist buses.

Madame Tussauds waxworks first came to London in 1802, after its eponymous creator was forced to flee the French Revolution, only narrowly escaping the guillotine herself by moulding death masks of the Revolution's victims. Madame Tussaud died in 1850 at the age of 89, and her last work, a self-portrait, is on display in the museum today.

An increasing number of Tussauds exhibits have some degree of interactivity involved – no doubt to fend off criticism of the otherwise unrealistic and static-looking mannequins. In **Blush** (an A-list party), **Premiere Nights** (which features superheros and iconic real people) and **World Stage** (covering world leaders, past and present, as well as top people from other fields) visitors can take pictures of themselves with all manner of celebrities – even the Queen.

New features are constantly replacing old ones as new

TV shows and personalities from all walks of life hit the headlines. Among the latest sections are a chance to confess in ***Big Brother's* Diary Room**, compete in **The X Factor** and board *Black Pearl* in **Pirates of the Caribbean**.

The famous **Chamber of Horrors** has been improved by a section with live actors: **Chamber Live!** (at extra cost and not for the nervous). Then mock black cabs in the

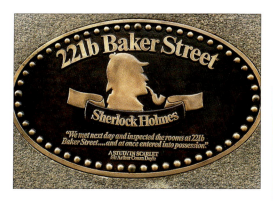

LONDON CENTRAL MOSQUE

On the western edge of Regent's Park, the **London Central Mosque** attests to the continuing religious and architectural diversity of the capital. Completed in 1978, it has a shining copper dome, a minaret and traditional Islamic interior décor. It can accommodate 1800 worshippers. Non-Muslim visitors should start at the information centre.

Spirit of London provide a whisk through four centuries of history. A visit to the **Stardome** rounds off the experience with an amusing Aardman Animations view of life on earth (sit at the back).

Sherlock Holmes Museum ★
Sir Arthur Conan Doyle's fictional Victorian detective, Sherlock Holmes, had his home at 221b Baker Street. The Sherlock Holmes Museum is a faithful reconstruction of his house as it might have been. It is, in fact, located at 239 Baker Street, even though the sign on the door says otherwise. Open daily 09:30–18:00. www.sherlock-holmes.co.uk

The British Library
After many delays, technical problems and overspending, the new British Library finally opened on Euston Road in 1997. It houses many millions of books and other printed works – over 150 million items and increasing by around 3 million every year. Here are displayed such national treasures as two of the surviving four copies of *Magna Carta*, the First Folio of Shakespeare's works, the beautiful 7th century *Lindisfarne Gospels*, the original manuscript of Lewis Caroll's *Alice in Wonderland* and the score of Handel's *Messiah*. Open 09:30–18:00 Mon, Wed, Thurs, Fri; 09:30–20:00 Tue; 09:30–17:00 Sat; 11:00–17:00 Sun. For visitor information, tel: (020) 7412 7332, www.bl.uk

REGENT'S CANAL

Running in a meandering path through north and east London down to the Thames at Limehouse, **Regent's Canal** was completed in 1820 and is still in use today. One of the most attractive sections is **Little Venice**, in Maida Vale (tube: Warwick Avenue) from where you can catch a **waterbus** down to **London Zoo** (which has its own jetty) and then on down to **Camden Lock**. The service runs hourly on the hour every day 10:00–17:00 Apr–Sep; less frequently Oct–Mar. Details from the London Waterbus Company, tel: (020) 7482 2660. **Jason's Canal Boats** do the same journey, with a commentary but without a zoo stop; tel: (020) 7286 3428, www.jasons.co.uk

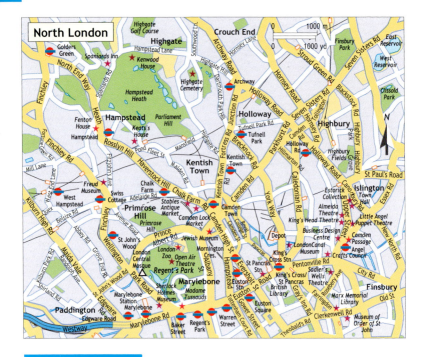

North London

Highgate
Golf Course
Highgate
Hampstead Lane
Crouch End
Golders
Green
Spaniards Inn
Kenwood
House
Highgate
Cemetery
Highgate
Hill
Archway
Holloway Road
Finsbury
Park
East
Reservoir
West
Reservoir
Clissold
Park
North End Way
Finchley
Hampstead
Heath
Holloway
Seven Sisters Rd
St Paul's Road
Fenton
House
Hampstead
Keats's
House
Parliament
Hill
Tufnell
Park
Highbury
Highbury
Fields
Freud
Museum
West
Hampstead
Swiss
Cottage
Chalk
Farm
Primrose
Hill
Camden
Town
Islington
Town
Hall
Estorick
Collection
Almeida
Theatre
Little Angel
Puppet Theatre
Kentish
Town
Stables
Antique
Market
Camden Lock
Market
St John's
Wood
London
Central
Mosque
London
Zoo
Open Air
Theatre
Jewish Museum
Mornington
Cres.
Business Design
Centre
LondonCanal
Museum
Camden
Passage
Angel
Crafts Council
Regent's Park
Marylebone
Sherlock
Holmes
Museum
Madame
Tussauds
Depot
King's
Cross Stn
St Pancras
Stn
King's Cross/
St Pancras
British
Library
Sadler's
Wells
Theatre
Finsbury
Marx Memorial
Library
Paddington
Edgware Road
Westway
Marylebone
Station
Marylebone Rd
Baker
Street
Regent's
Park
Warren
Street
Euston
Square
Euston
Stn
Clerkenwell Rd
Museum of
Order of St
John

0　　　1000 m
0　　　1000 yd

ST JOHN'S WOOD

Smart residential **St John's Wood** is home to England's most famous cricket venue, **Lord's Cricket Ground**, which is owned by the Marylebone Cricket Club (MCC). Tours of the ground and museum are available most days at 12:00 and 14:00 all year, plus 10:00 Apr–Sept; tel: (020) 7616 8595, www.lords.org Nearby is **Abbey Road Studios** where the **Beatles** recorded much of their work during the 1960s. For guided tours of Beatles' London, contact Original London Walks, tel: (020) 7624 3978, www.walks.com

REGENT'S PARK

Extending north from Marylebone Road up towards Hampstead and Camden, Regent's Park is best known as the home of London Zoo, and for the elegant Regency terraces (designed by John Nash) which surround it. It was once a thickly wooded area (and the private hunting grounds of Henry VIII) until Cromwell felled most of its 1600 trees to help build ships for the Navy.

Nash and the Prince Regent (later George IV) envisaged a belt of grand terraced houses around the outside of the park, and although the scheme was never completed, Nash's legacy is still visible in the cream-coloured stucco of **Chester Terrace** and **Cumberland Terrace**, and the architecturally diverse houses of **Park Village West**. The **Open-Air Theatre** in the Inner Circle was popular in the 1930s for its productions of *A Midsummer Night's Dream*, and the summer repertoire still includes

Shakespeare. The nearby **Queen Mary's Gardens** have one of the country's best rose displays. Beyond Prince Albert Row is **Primrose Hill**, well worth the climb to enjoy sweeping panoramas of the city.

London Zoo ★★

Covering 14ha (34½ acres) of the northern corner of Regent's Park, the London Zoo has endured its fair share of ups and downs – including threats of complete closure due to funding problems – since it was first opened by the Zoological Society of London in 1828, making it one of the world's oldest and not to be compared with more modern zoos elsewhere in the world. It has, however, long been at the forefront of zoological studies and scientific research into animal genetics, ecology, behaviour and reproduction, and can claim many firsts, including the public aquarium (1849), the reptile house (1853), the insect house (1881), and a children's zoo (1938).

The complex includes themed areas such as **Into Africa**, where you look down on African hunting dogs and warthogs, admire okapis and can watch giraffes from a platform at *their* eye level; **Gorilla Kingdom**, which recreates the gorillas' natural habitat; the **Small Mammals House** – a two-storey rainforest featuring such creatures as marmosets and agoutis; and the attractive new **Penguin Pool**, packed at feeding time.

There's plenty to enjoy elsewhere, from tiny endangered tree snails in the **Invertebrate House** to Sumatran tigers. Kids can get hands-on in the **Ambika Paul Children's Zoo** and a variety of birds and animals show off their special skills in **Animals in Action** shows. Open daily with slight variations, but essentially: 10:00–16:30 Easter–Oct; 10:00–15:00 Oct–Easter. www.londonzoo.co.uk

Below: *The Snowdon Aviary rises up majestically alongside Regent's Canal at London Zoo.*

CAMDEN PUBS

Camden has a proliferation
of good pubs, many of them
with live music and most
packed to overflowing at
weekends. Some open only
in the evenings. Among the
more popular are **Oxford
Arms** (a traditional pub with
a beer garden and good bar
food) and the **Fusilier and
Firkin** (excellent locally
brewed beers, good food and
live music).

CAMDEN TOWN

Another of London's more Bohemian 'village suburbs',
Camden Town is popular among Londoners for its extensive **markets**, of which there are several at either side of
Camden Lock on the Regent's Canal. You may well find
designer clothes here before they become household
names. At weekends it buzzes with activity and scores of
shops, trendy pubs, bistros and restaurants complement
the markets, each with their own character and style. Most
of the markets open daily 10:00–17:00 or longer.

The original **Camden Market** has around 120 stalls
where the emphasis is mostly on fashion, jewellery, and
great second-hand clothing, music and food. Between
this market and Camden Town tube is the indoor
Electric Ballroom Market (Sun only), which features up-
and-coming fashion and jewellery designers. Opposite
here, the **Inverness Street Market** is the oldest section,
and sells fruit and vegetables.

On the other side of the canal
bridge the **Camden Lock Market**,
with many exotic food stalls, is
the main arts and crafts area, with
the many small boutiques and
craft workshops supplemented at
weekends by hundreds of stalls
selling bric-a-brac, candles,
prints, books, clothes, period
clothing and much more besides.

Between Camden Town tube
and Chalk Farm tube, **Camden
High Street** and **Chalk Farm Road**
(its extension) is the main drag, a
mile long and lined with a variety
of interesting stores, from bookshops and galleries to specialist
craft shops and plenty of trendy
shoes, shades and clothes.

On Chalk Farm Road is the
Stables Antique Market which is
the biggest of all the markets,

Left: *Camden Lock, terminus for canal cruises, is filled with little arty shops and stalls.*
Opposite: *St Pancras Station, one of London's most exuberant Victorian buildings.*

and has some of the best bargains in collectables and antiques, ornaments, furniture, as well as good quality second-hand clothes.

Comparatively unknown, but growing in interest, is **Camden Canal Market** (Fri–Sun only), with some 150 varied stalls/shops and international take-away food.

Within a few minutes' walk of Camden Town tube is the **Jewish Museum** at 129 Albert Street, which has a series of stylish galleries on Jewish religious life and history in Britain, and a renowned ceremonial art collection; there are also interesting audiovisual displays explaining the Jewish faith and customs. It includes treasures from London's Great Synagogue which was burnt down during the Second World War. Open 10:00–15:30 Mon–Thu, 10:00–16:30 Sun; closed on bank and Jewish holidays. www.jewishmuseum.org.uk

To the south of Camden Town, the area around **King's Cross** railway station, once a notorious red-light district, is currently undergoing extensive redevelopment as a terminal for the Channel tunnel trains. Alongside King's Cross the old **St Pancras** station, with its magnificent mock-Gothic spires, is a marvel of Victorian architecture. The modern **British Library** is beside it (*see* p. 83).

Behind King's Cross, canal boats moor up in the King's Cross Basin, where the interesting little **London Canal Museum** traces the social and commercial history of canal boats – and of ice cream. Open 10:00–16:30 Tue–Sun and holiday Mon. www.canalmuseum.org.uk

PUPPET SHOWS

Founded in 1961, the **Little Angel Theatre**, 14 Dagmar Passage, Islington, is London's only permanent puppet theatre. It is aimed primarily, but not exclusively, at children, and features all types of puppets. The venue is often used by touring puppet companies, tel: (020) 7226 1787 or visit www.littleangeltheatre.com

The **Puppet Theatre Barge**, going since 1982, uses both marionettes and rod puppets, in a 50-seat auditorium on a narrowboat. In winter it's based in Little Venice (135 Bloomfield Road); in summer it moors at various sites along the Thames, tel: (020) 7249 6876. www.puppetbarge.com

Above: *The elegant, white-washed façade of Keats's former home in Hampstead.*

HAMPSTEAD

Hampstead was first recorded in the Domesday Book as 'Hampstede', meaning homestead, and consisted of nothing more than a small rural farm. By the 18th century it had become a fashionable spa, selling water to city-dwellers in the aptly named **Flask Walk**, and later became (as it still is) a popular residence for the wealthy, the intelligentsia and literary set.

Hampstead's steeply sloping village **High Street** features numerous fashion shops, art and antiques galleries, boutiques and craft shops, as well as arty cafés and lively pubs. Surrounding it is a maze of cobblestone lanes, alleyways, elegant houses and Georgian squares.

Hampstead Museums ★

Before heading off to the wide open spaces of Hampstead Heath, there are several noteworthy museums in the vicinity. The **Freud Museum,** 20 Maresfield Gardens, (open 12:00–17:00, Wed–Sun) is where Freud lived after escaping from the Nazis in 1938, until his death the following year. His library and study (including the famous couch) have been preserved and the house contains his collection of erotic antiquities and archives. www.freud.org.uk

At **Keats's House**, Keats Grove, Wentworth Place, the poet is commemorated in the house where he lived 1818–20. The Regency villa contains a collection of his books, manuscripts, letters and personal possessions. It was here he created *Ode to a Nightingale* and fell in love with his neighbour, Fanny Brawne. Open 13:00–17:00 Tue–Sat and holiday Mon. www.keatshouse.org.uk

Music aficionados should head for **Fenton House**, where the collection of old instruments includes a 1612 harpsichord played by Handel. Open Easter–Oct: 14:00–16:30 Wed–Fri; 11:00–16:30 Sat–Sun and holiday Mon. Frequent summer concerts on Thu. For more information, tel: (020) 7435 3471. www.nationaltrust.org.uk

SPANIARDS INN

To the west of Kenwood House at the northern end of Spaniards Road, traffic is forced to slow down as it negotiates a narrow passage between an old toll booth and the historic **Spaniards Inn**, an 18th-century coaching inn. The famous highwayman Dick Turpin is said to have used it as a hiding place and to spy out likely looking coaches to rob as they left London on the road north. Legend has it that he would fire his pistol nightly as a signal at closing time.

Hampstead Heath **

Hampstead's main attraction is the 300ha (741-acre) expanse of the Heath, one of the most popular parks in London, with woodlands, open fields, heathland, and 28 natural ponds (some are used for swimming or fishing). For great views of Hampstead and the City head for **Parliament Hill**, which is a popular spot for kite-flying. On the northern fringes of the

Heath is **Kenwood House**, a 17th-century mansion with a noteworthy interior remodelled by Robert Adam – his library is a highlight. The house now contains the **Iveagh Bequest**, a fabulous collection featuring such artists as Vermeer, Rembrandt, Reynolds and Gainsborough. Open daily 11:00–17:00 Apr–Oct; 11:00–16:00 Nov–Mar. In summer there are frequent concerts by the lake, featuring a variety of musical genres. For details of performances, tel: (020) 8348 1286. www.english-heritage.org.uk

Above: *Hampstead Heath is one of the most pleasant of London's parks by day. At night it's a noted pick-up area for gay men.*

HIGHGATE

While not as prestigious as neighbouring Hampstead, Highgate has still had its share of famous residents (including Sir Francis Bacon and Samuel Coleridge), and can boast one of London's most famous graves, that of **Karl Marx**. Highgate (named after the country's oldest tollgate which once stood in the present-day High Street) is visited mainly for the extraordinary **Cemetery**, with its mausoleums, catacombs, and bizarre statuary. Others buried here include Christina Rossetti, Charles Dickens's wife Catherine, and author Mary Ann Evans (a.k.a. George Eliot).

The **West Cemetery** is the most interesting part, containing impressive vaults and statuary. It can be visited only on a tour: hourly 11:00–16:00 Sat–Sun; also Mon–Fri at 14:00 if sufficient demand, so book on tel: (020) 8340 1834. www.highgate-cemetery.org

FAMOUS RESIDENTS

Almost every street in Hampstead seems to have blue plaques commemorating famous residents of the past: William Blake, Agatha Christie, Richard Burton, George Orwell, Robert Louis Stevenson, John Constable, Charles de Gaulle, John le Carré, Henry Moore, Peter Sellers, AA Milne, Edith Sitwell and Barbara Hepworth are just some of them. More recently, it has been home to celebrities such as Elizabeth Taylor, Sting, Boy George, Tom Conti, Emma Thompson, and Jeremy Irons, to name but a few.

Right: *Colourful barges at Islington Lock on the Regent's Canal, a pleasant way to travel through parts of North London.* **Opposite:** *St John's Gate (16th century) is one of the three medieval establishments that survive today.*

INTERESTING WALKS

Islington and Clerkenwell are fascinating areas best explored on foot and there are two excellent local companies to consult. Both offer some regular strolls and other themed walks on request, so call them for precise details.
  Local historian and lecturer Peter Powell leads **Angel Walks**, with literary and historic themes: tel: (07796) 673 846, www.angelwalks.co.uk
  The **Clerkenwell & Islington Guides Association** cover Clerkenwell (11:00 Wed, 14:00 Sat), The Angel Islington (14:00 Sun) and Smithfield (14:00 Sun); tel: (020) 7622 3278, www.clerkenwellwalks.org.uk

ISLINGTON

Islington was a spa resort that developed into a working class district. In the 1970s an influx of writers, media folk and left-leaning trendies led to today's lively mix of bistros, ethnic restaurants, quirky shops and unusual theatre venues. The **Almeida**, one of London's premier showcases for new talent, alternates classics and new plays. Islington is also home to one of the best of many small theatre companies attached to pubs, the renowned **King's Head**. These venues are far cheaper than the West End theatres but the shows are often just as good.

Islington also has a top-notch gallery in the form of the **Estorick Collection of Modern Italian Art**. The collection, which is housed in a Grade II listed Georgian building in Canonbury Square, is known internationally for its core of Futuristic works as well as figurative art and sculpture dating from 1850 to the 1950s. It features paintings by Futurism's main protagonists such as Balla, Boccioni, Carra, Russolo and Severini. Open 11:00–18:00 Wed–Sat, 12:00–17:00 Sun.
www.estorickcollection.com

Regent's Canal emerges from a tunnel at the bottom of Duncan Street. Access to the towpath is from Colebrooke Row and it's possible to follow it all the way to Limehouse: with breaks at some interesting pubs along the way.

Camden Passage **

Islington's main attraction is the **antiques market**, which is located just a few minutes' walk from Angel tube. It fills Camden Passage on Wed mornings and Sat, but the surrounding antique shops are open every day of the week. **Chapel Market** (open Tue–Sun), on the other side of Upper Street, is traditional London food and dry goods market.

CLERKENWELL

Situated between Holborn and Islington, Clerkenwell has long been associated with craft industries and the opulent displays of **Hatton Garden** (off Holborn Circus), testify that it is still the main centre in the United Kingdom for the gemstone trade, while its other role as a centre of radical politics is reflected by the presence of the **Marx Memorial Library** on Clerkenwell Green. The library is only open to non-members 13:00–14:00 Mon–Thu.
www.marxlibrary.net

Museum of the Order of St John *

The crusading Knights Hospitallers were based here and the remains of their 13th-century priory are to the southeast of Clerkenwell Green. The most conspicuous remnant is **St John's Gate**, now containing a museum about the Order and St John's Ambulance. Open 10:00–17:00, Mon–Fri; 10:00–16:00 Sat but closed Sat–Mon on holiday weekends. To see the **Grand Priory crypt** and the rooms inside the **Gatehouse** and **Chapter Hall**, you must join a tour (11:00 and 14:30 Tue, Fri, Sat). ww.sja.org.uk/museum

Charterhouse *

A few minutes' walk from St John's Gate is Charterhouse, a 14th–17th-century Carthusian monastery. The complex includes monks' cells and Renaissance ornamentation in the Great Hall and Great Chamber. It can be visited by pre-booked tour on Wed afternoons Apr–Aug. For information, tel: (020) 7251 5002.

LITTLE ITALY

In the 19th century Italian immigrants were in demand for their skills as painters, artisans and also dancing and fencing teachers. They established their own **Little Italy** in Clerkenwell around Rosebery Avenue, Farringdon Road and Clerkenwell Road. Its focal point was **St Peter's Italian Church** and though nowadays the 10,000 Italians who originally lived here have settled elsewhere, there are still Italian restaurants, delicatessens and wine merchants in the vicinity.

MOUNT PLEASANT

Post offices don't normally feature much as tourist attractions but the **Mount Pleasant Sorting Office** – the largest in the country – is unique in that it has its own private underground railway system which shuttles down a network of tunnels to other sorting offices, a miniature (and driverless) version of the tube. Viewing is by arrangement; tel: (020) 7239 2312.

8
South of the Thames

London's traditional draws are mostly north of the Thames and many visitors are unaware of the riches to be found along the south bank. Pedestrian access to this side of the Thames has become much easier thanks to the fantastic **Millenium Bridge** reaching across from St Paul's to Bankside, and two new pedestrian bridges either side of the **Hungerford Bridge** which spans the river from Charing Cross to the South Bank Centre. The **South Bank Centre** is Europe's largest arts complex and includes the **Royal National Theatre** and **National Film Theatre**.

A little to the south, what was the old **County Hall** has recently developed into another entertainment centre: from the elegant **British Airways London Eye** to the extraordinary **Dalí Universe** and superb **London Aquarium**. Further south, **Lambeth's** attractions include the excellent **Imperial War Museum** and a charming **Museum of Garden History**.

Heading in the other direction, you reach the offbeat shops and other attractions of the **Oxo Tower Wharf** and, beyond them, **Bankside**, where the vast **Tate Modern** provides a complete contrast to the reconstruction of Shakespeare's **Globe Theatre**. Beyond Southwark Bridge, there's **Vinopolis** – a must for lovers of wine – and ancient **Southwark Cathedral**. Continuing east, the horrors of the ever-popular **London Dungeon** attract long queues, while *HMS Belfast* can easily accommodate hordes of visitors. The last stretch is **Butler's Wharf**, just east of Tower Bridge, where the interesting **Design Museum** and **Fashion and Textile Museum** are sited.

Opposite: *The Imperial War Museum.*

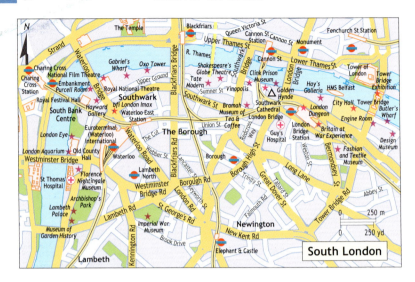

South London

As Westminster began to emerge as the focus for political and royal power in the 13th century, the clergy decided they had to have a presence nearby, so the Bishop of Winchester built **Southwark Palace** (of which little remains), and the then Archbishop of Canterbury built **Lambeth Palace**, which is still the Archbishop's London residence. This palace is seldom open to the public.

Right: *The attractive Tudor Gatehouse at Lambeth Palace.*
Opposite: *The Royal Festival Hall is located at the South Bank Centre.*

LAMBETH

Imperial War Museum ★★

Twentieth-century warfare in all its aspects (including its impact on civilians) is the subject of this museum, presented in atmospheric sections covering specific themes. The vast **entrance hall** is full of real weapons and vehicles, from a tank to a Spitfire. The **two World War**

galleries cover all the fronts, and offer a walk-through WWI trench (complete with effects). **Children at War** is a wonderfully evocative gallery with a recreated 30s/40s house; the harrowing **Holocaust Exhibition** (with scale model of Auschwitz and audio-visual reminiscences of survivors) evokes the horrors of anti-Semitism; and **Secret War** concentrates on espionage. The museum is free, but there are fees for special exhibitions – invariably worthwhile. Open 10:00–18:00 daily all year. www.iwm.org.uk

Florence Nightingale Museum *

On a corner of St Thomas's Hospital, where the 'Lady with the Lamp' set up the first professional school of nursing, is her memorial, with audio-visual presentations and recreations of the Crimean hospitals. Open 10:00–16:00 Mon–Fri, 10:00–14:30 Sat–Sun. www.florence-nightingale.co.uk

Museum of Garden History *

Next door to Lambeth Palace, inside a deconsecrated church are displays on the development of garden design and early plant hunters (such as 17th-century Royal Gardener, John Tradescant, who travelled widely to bring new species back to Britain). Outside, there is a period garden with, unexpectedly, the sarcophagus of Captain Bligh of *Mutiny on the Bounty* fame. Open 10:30–17:00 daily, Jan to mid-Dec. www.museumgardenhistory.org

DUCK TOURS

Departing from County Hall on the South Bank every half hour, the 70 minute Duck Tour offers an unusual perspective on the sights of the city, with an amphibious craft which drives past the famous landmarks before launching itself into the river for the waterborne section of the tour. The vehicles, known as DUKWS, were first used in the D-Day landings. Tel: (020) 7928 3132; www.londonducktours.co.uk

RIB VOYAGES

A truly different way to view the river is by 12-seater rubber inflatable boat (RIB). Voyages start tamely (with a commentary) but, once past Tower Bridge, they become an exhilarating white-water ride, as the RIBS cut across the wake of larger vessels and execute sharp U-turns. Departures from Waterloo (London Eye) pier. Daily (weather permitting) 11:15–16:15. To book, tel: (020) 7401 8834 or 7928 2350. www.londonribvoyages.com

OXO TOWER WHARF

The Oxo Tower's rooftop restaurant offers superb views and stays open late evening, tel: (020) 7803 3888, as well as a variety of design stores open 11:00–18:00 Tue–Sun and a gallery with changing exhibitions, open daily 11:00–18:00. www.oxotower.co.uk

Above: *The London Eye pro-vides an overview the city.*
Opposite: *The Globe Theatre.*

COUNTY HALL
London Aquarium ★★

Suitably positioned beside the Thames, in County Hall, the Aquarium is on two levels. Do not take the escalator up from the lower level until you are ready to leave: there is no way back. The place is split into geographical areas and tanks recreate all the different watery habitats to be found on earth, from freshwater streams to the ocean depths. Open daily 10:00–18:00 (summer) 17:00 (winter). www.londonaqaurium.co.uk

Dalí Universe ★★

Also housed in County Hall, this intriguing museum presents a collection of bizarre paintings, sculptures, graphics, jewellery and furniture created by the eccentric Spanish Surrealist, Salvador Dalí. Open daily 10:00–17:30. www.daliuniverse.com

British Airways London Eye ★★★

Visible for miles, the Eye has quickly become London's most popular paid attraction. It soars 135m (450ft) above the Thames, the glass capsules providing unrivalled all-round views. 'Flights' last about 30min, 10:00–21:00 Jun–Sep; 10:00–20:00 Oct–May. Book at County Hall, or tel: (0870) 500 0600. For a 10% discount visit www.ba-londoneye.com

THE SOUTH BANK
South Bank Centre ★★

The vast range of arts staged at the South Bank Centre make it one of the main cultural hubs of the city. The centre developed after the 1951 Festival of Britain, a post-war effort to boost morale, with the South Bank Exhibition as its centrepiece. The oldest building in the complex is the **Royal Festival Hall** (RFH), which is undergoing a £70m redevelopment programme, due for completion in 2008. The RFH is one of the capital's main concert venues, with the London Philharmonic as its resident orchestra. The other main concert halls are the **Queen Elizabeth Hall** and the more intimate **Purcell Room**. Behind these venues is the **Hayward Gallery** (open daily 10:00–18:00, closing 20:00 Tue–Wed), easily located by the tall neon sculpture on its roof. The Hayward hosts major art exhibitions. The **National Theatre** (NT) has three main auditoriums (the Olivier, Lyttelton and Cottesloe) and constantly experiments with other spaces, inside and al fresco, to provide an outstanding variety of productions, conventional and otherwise. Then there is the **National Film Theatre** (NFT), which has four auditoriums where over 2000 films are screened each year, and workshops and lectures are hosted. The nearby **bfi London IMAX Cinema** boasts the largest screen in Britain: the height of a ten-storey building. www.bfi.org.uk

BANKSIDE
Shakespeare's Globe Exhibition ★★★

The Globe Theatre is a faithful recreation of the original structure of the early 1600s – the first thatched building in the capital since the Great Fire of London. In summer (May–Sep), Shakespeare's works are presented as they would have been in his day (but with actresses). The techniques are best appreciated if you take the tour before attending a performance. A permanent exhibition (entrance in an adjacent building) uses a combination of modern technology and traditional skills to cover Bankside, Shakespeare and his theatres, actors and audiences, as well as Sam Wanamaker's struggle to recreate the Globe. A tour of the theatre is included when it is not in use – when it is, a visit to the site of Shakespeare's original Rose Theatre is substituted. Open daily 10:00–17:00 (with Globe) Oct–Apr; 09:00–12:00 (with Globe) and 12:30–17:00 (with Rose) May–Sep. www.shakespeares-globe.org

THE GLOBE THEATRE

Shakespeare's plays were written for his theatre on the banks of the Thames, known as the 'Wooden O', and it was here that *King Lear*, *Macbeth*, *Hamlet*, *Othello* and many other productions were first staged. It was closed down by the Puritans in 1642. The current recreation is largely due to the American film-maker Sam Wanamaker, who came to London in 1949 expecting to find a Globe Theatre and, disappointed, set about raising funds to rebuild it; he died in 1993, but his vision has been realized. A full performance season in the half-covered theatre (which holds an audience of 1500) began in 1997.

GABRIEL'S WHARF

This is a pleasant little enclave full of eateries and craft shops: you can often watch such things as jewellery and ceramics being created.

FASHION AND TEXTILE MUSEUM

The Fashion and Textile Museum is the first museum in Britain dedicated to contemporary fashion and textiles. The focus is on international fashion and textile design from 1950 to the present day and includes works by Biba, Ossie Clark, Bill Gibb, Jean Muir, Christain Dior and others. The core collection comprises over 3000 original garments donated by the museum's founder, designer Zandra Rhodes, along with archive material and show videos. It is currently open only to pre-booked small groups. Tel: (020) 7407 8664. www.ftmlondon.org

GOLDEN HYNDE

Moored in Clink Street is an accurate, full-sized reconstruction of Sir Francis Drake's 16th-century warship, Golden Hynde. This Tudor galleon is a living history museum, with a full time schedule of educational programmes and guided tours. The ship, built in 1973, is a seaworthy vessel and has itself circumnavigated the globe. There are exhibits and artefacts on each of her five decks, including 14 canons on the gun deck. For details of tours, workshops and other events, tel: (0870) 011 8700.

Tate Modern ***

What was once an ugly power station is now a stunning architectural mix of new and old, with stupendous views from the 7th-floor café. Much of the Tate's enormous collection had been languishing unseen for decades, due to lack of space. Now, at last, hundreds of paintings and sculptures are once again on view. Arranged by subject, rather than style or chronology, there are four themed galleries which enable viewers to appreciate the changing styles of the 20th century. Films and televisions are scattered through the building to lend an extra dimension and long-established favourites (such as Monet's *Water Lilies* and Rodin's *The Kiss*) mingle with controversial new works. Open 10:00–17:15 Sun–Thu, 10:00–21:15 Fri–Sat. www.tate.org.uk

An enjoyable way to travel between Tate Modern and Tate Britain (*see* p. 35) is on the Tate Boat, which runs between them every 40 min, also stopping at the London Eye. Buy tickets at the pier.

SOUTHWARK
Southwark Cathedral **

Although it has been a cathedral only since 1905, the building is rich in history, having grown from a 13th-century church which incorporated part of a Roman villa: an interesting audio tour of the cathedral is available. Parts of a genuine dig exposing several periods can be seen in the passage between the cathedral and the exhibition. Open 08:00–18:00 Mon–Fri, 09:00–18:00 Sat–Sun, but no audio tours during services. www.dswark.org/cathedral

Vinopolis **

Not to be missed by wine lovers, Vinopolis (Bank End/ Clink Street: signposted from the riverside) is devoted to the wines of the world, with audio tours of regions and their history. You can travel through the themed areas at your own pace and the entry fee includes five tastings of wine plus a cocktail. It also features a Still Room for lovers of Scotch whisky. Entry 12:00–19:00 Mon, Fri–Sat, 12:00–16:00 Sun, Tue–Thu. An art gallery, wine shop and excellent restaurant are also on offer. www.vinopolis.co.uk

Clink Prison Museum ★★

Clink Prison is a small but atmospheric recreation in what remains of a real 12th-century prison, which has given its name as a slang term for all prisons. The guided tour is recommended. Open 10:00–18:00 Mon–Fri, 10:00–21:00 Sat–Sun. www.clink.co.uk

POOL OF LONDON
HMS Belfast ★★

The largest surviving battle cruiser from World War II, *HMS Belfast* remained in service until 1965 and is now a floating museum, moored just upstream from Tower Bridge. This complex warship (which carried 800 crew) has nine decks and you can explore all of it, from the bridge down to the engine and boiler rooms. Open daily 10:00–17:15 Mar–Oct; 10:00–16:15 Nov–Feb. www.iwm.org.uk

The London Dungeon ★★

Housed in vaults on Tooley Street, the dungeon is a macabre look at the gruesome aspects of history, with life-size tableaux (some animatronic) of people being beheaded, drawn and quartered, hanged, etc. Jack the Ripper's London, the Great Fire, the Plague and a boat ride through Traitor's Gate are all features. Open daily 09:30/ 10:30–17:00/18:00. Immensely popular, so be prepared to queue. www.thedungeons.com

HAY'S GALLERIA

Between London Bridge station and the river, **Hay's Galleria** is an unusual shopping precinct built over the former Hay's Dock with a curved glass-and-steel roof enclosing the warehouses on either side. It contains continental-style shops, bars and restaurants.

SOUTHWARK TIC

The Southwark Tourist Information Centre is looking for permanent premises in the area, but can be reached on tel: (020) 7357 9168. www.visitsouthwark.com

Below: *The London Dungeon offers London's most grisly entertainment and attracts vast crowds.*

BUTLER'S WHARF

This was one of London's busiest 19th-century docks, handling goods from around the world. Porters trundled loads over cobbled streets and along aerial walkways that linked the warehouses. Skilfully rejuvenated by Terence Conran, founder of Habitat, the wharf is now home to upmarket galleries, restaurants and food shops.

CITY HALL

A spectacular lopsided glass building beside Tower Bridge is the new home of the GLA and Mayor of London. There's public access, but the viewing platform is usually open only in the first weekend of the month, so check: tel: (020) 7983 4000 – or the Events Calendar on www.london.gov.uk

Britain at War Experience **

Just along from the London Dungeon, this evocative theme museum conveys the atmosphere of wartime London and how people coped during the Blitz (rationing, blackouts, etc.).

It starts with a creaking elevator ride into an air-raid shelter and ends with a realistic mock-up of a bombed-out, rubble-strewn street, complete with special effects such as smells and smoke. Open daily all year from 10:00–17:00, Apr–Sep at 10:00–16:00 and Oct–Mar. www.britainatwar.co.uk

BUTLER'S WHARF
Design Museum **

This museum, at Butler's Wharf, provides a revealing insight into design as it relates to everyday objects such as cars and furniture.

There are both permanent and temporary exhibitions and displays include some products not yet in production. Open daily 10:00–17:15 all year. www.designmuseum.org

Bramah Tea and Coffee Museum *

Situated in Southwark Street is an interesting little museum covering three centuries of the social and commercial history of the world's two most favourite hot beverages.

After admiring the exhibits, including several teapots in a variety of amusing designs, you can sample the brew of your choice in the small café on the premises, where traditional English afternoon tea is served from 14:00–16:00. Open daily all year from 10:00–18:00. ww.bramahmuseum.co.uk

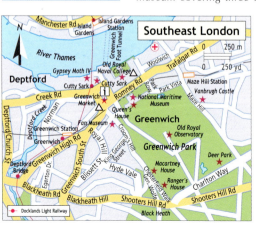

Left: *Parts of Wren's Royal Naval College are open to the public, except during special functions.*

GREENWICH

One of London's most attractive villages, Greenwich makes a pleasant excursion along the Thames – or you can take the Docklands Light Railway (DLR) to Cutty Sark station, which is a better option for sightseeing than Greenwich station.

National Maritime Museum ★★★

In addition to the usual paintings, models of large ships and actual presence of small vessels, from Prince Frederick's gilded barge to a Modern Olympics 49er, the museum offers working models, specialist galleries devoted to such things as exploration of the deep and plenty of educational audio-visual displays. **Nelson's Navy** includes fascinating personal details, as well as covering his public life. **All Hands** is full of simple hands-on machines for kids, while children of all ages enjoy **The Bridge**, where an excellent simulation enables them to try their hand at navigating a vessel. Open daily 10:00–17:30 Jul–Aug; 10:00–16:30 Sep–Jun. www.nmm.ac.uk

The adjoining **Queen's House**, designed by Inigo Jones, now houses changing exhibitions of pictures from the Maritime Museum's collection, including Turner's magnificent depiction of the Battle of Trafalgar. Open daily 10:00–16:30.

TIME IN GREENWICH

During the early 19th century most parts of Britain ran on different time zones. This was fine during the days of stage-coach travel, but it made the timetables of the newly emerging rail network particularly confusing. From 1852 London time was adopted as standard, but clocks still showed both local and London time; this continued until 1884 when Greenwich Mean Time (GMT) was adopted as the standard by which not just Britain but the whole world set its clocks. An international convention placed Longitude 0 degrees (the imaginary line joining the North and South Poles) at Greenwich, and by standing on this Meridian (an illuminated line on the ground) at the Old Royal Observatory you are straddling the eastern and western hemispheres. The red time ball on top of Flamsteed House (the old observatory) is raised and dropped every day – as it has been for over a century – at 13:00 as a time signal to shipping on the River Thames.

Below: *The Royal Observatory has set the standard for global time for over three centuries.*

The Old Royal Naval College ★★

Highlights of Wren's Royal Naval College are the magnificent **Painted Hall**, with decorations that took nearly 20 years to complete, and the elegant **Chapel**, where concerts and recitals are regularly performed. Open 10:00–17:00 daily. www.greenwichfoundation.org.uk

The Old Royal Observatory ★★

Built in 1676 for Charles II's Royal Astronomer, the Old Royal Observatory sits atop the hill in Greenwich Park on the Greenwich Meridian line, and has an interesting display on time and astronomy, with old telescopes and other instruments. One of the exhibits is the first marine chronometer, probably 'the most important timepiece ever made' since it enabled ships to calculate longitude, and so navigate accurately for the first time. Open daily 10:00–16:30/17:30 (seasonal). There's a stunning view over Greenwich Park and Queen Anne's House to Canary Wharf, with *Cutty Sark*'s rigging to the left and the **Millennium Dome** to the right. www.nmm.ac.uk

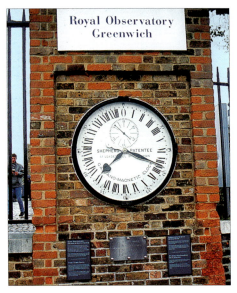

A new **Time and Space Centre** concentrates on astronomy and includes a 120-seat state-of-the-art **Planetarium**.

Cutty Sark ★★

On board the *Cutty Sark* are the original gilded teak fittings, the rigging on its three masts, and a lot of maritime memorabilia. The below-decks area houses colourful figureheads, and some cabins above contain tableaux of what ship life was like. Built on the Clyde in 1869, the *Cutty Sark* was one of the last tea clippers, fast sailing ships which competed each year to bring the first of the new tea crop back from China.

A £13-million conservation project will occupy most of 2007 (possibly longer) but 'Hard Hat Tours' will be available until *Cutty Sark* reopens with improved facilities. For information, tel: (020) 8858 3445. www.cuttysark.org.uk

Fan Museum

This delightful museum, a few minutes' walk from the pier, at 12 Crooms Hill, has changing themed exhibitions formed by displaying some unusual fans from a collection of around 3000. Open 11:00–17:00, Tue–Sat; 12:00–17:00 Sun; closed Mon. www.fan-museum.org

Above: *The Thames Barrier at Woolwich, built to counteract the ever-increasing danger of floods caused by global warming.*

WOOLWICH
The Thames Barrier ★

London has always lived with the threat of flooding from the Thames. A flood barrier was first proposed in the 19th century, but it wasn't until the 1980s that one was actually built – a unique and impressive structure it is too, with its ten massive stainless steel gates, each weighing 3700 tonnes, which take half-an-hour to be raised or lowered. They have been used to prevent floods more than 90 times since being completed, and are tested every month. For schedules, tel: (020) 8305 4188. There are good views of the structure from the visitors centre. Open daily 10:30–16:00 April to September, 11:00–15:30 October to March. For a clear view of the barrier from the river, take a boat trip from Greewich.

Woolwich Railway Museum ★

The Railway Museum, Pier Road, is a must for all railway enthusiasts. It is located at the old Railway Station and depicts the history of the Great Eastern Railway, founded in 1862, and includes some restored steam engines. Open daily 13:00–17:00 in local (i.e. Newham) school holidays, but Sat–Sun only during other months (closed in December). To check times, tel: (020) 7474 7244.

MILITARY WOOLWICH

Woolwich has a long history as a military depot, starting with the creation of the **Royal Dockyards** in 1513 by Henry VIII. Sir Walter Raleigh and Captain Cook set out on their voyages from the docks here, which eventually closed in 1869. The buildings of the **Royal Arsenal** (where gunpowder was manufactured in the 17th century) now house the multimedia **FirePower** – a Royal Artillery museum that recreates the experiences of 20th-century gunners and the history of artillery. Open 10:30–16:00 Wed–Sun Apr–Oct; 10:30–16:00 Fri–Sun Nov–Mar. www.firepower.org.uk

9
Nearby Excursions

Barnes, the area south of Hammersmith Bridge, is home to the award-winning **London Wetlands Centre**. An enjoyable riverside walk leads west from the north side of the bridge, past several popular pubs, including the 17th-century **The Dove**, to the village of Chiswick, noted for historic riverside pubs and the splendours of **Chiswick House**.

As the River Thames loops its way southwards, it passes through **Kew** and **Richmond**, affluent suburbs which have enjoyed Royal patronage from the 12th century, when palaces were built here on the riverbanks. The fabulous **Kew Gardens** is one of the chief legacies of the old royal estates, as is the walled **Richmond Park**, where herds of deer roam among the bracken and coppices. Other attractions include stately mansions such as **Syon House** and **Osterley House**.

Still further to the southwest is **Hampton Court**, one of the greatest of the Royal palaces, with wonderfully opulent rooms hidden away behind its red-brick exterior. The magnificent gardens add to the allure of this vast palace, which is well worth the 20km (12½ mile) journey out from the centre of town.

And, of course, no visit to London would be complete without a trip to **Windsor Castle**, although it is some 40km (25 miles) from the city centre. A palpable sense of nearly a thousand years of history pervades this towered and turreted complex on a hilltop above the Thames. You can tour the royal apartments and view some of the superb Royal Collection.

DON'T MISS

*** **Hampton Court Palace** and **Windsor Castle:** royal residences filled with history.
*** **Kew Gardens:** visit the charmingly-restored Kew Palace, as well as the Gardens.
*** **London Wetlands Centre, Barnes:** a wonderful habitat for waterfowl.
** **Syon** and **Osterley House:** lordly riverbank mansions.
** **Richmond Park:** vast royal hunting grounds.
* **Chiswick:** traditional pub lunches beside the Thames and Chiswick House.

Opposite: *Henry VIII's magnificent Tudor palace at Hampton Court.*

LONDON WETLANDS CENTRE

Across the Thames from Hammersmith were the London reservoirs. When they became obsolete, conservationists created a 43ha (106-acre) wetlands reserve, the **London Wetlands Centre**, Queen Elizabeth's Walk, tel: (020) 8409–4400.

Combining special habitats with a large wildlife area has provided a haven for over 150 species of bird (some on the verge of extinction). Strategically positioned hides, 'Field Notes', interactive games and a visitor centre complete with an excellent café are available.

Open daily, 09:30–17:00 in summer, closes an hour earlier Oct–Mar. From the bus station at Hammersmith tube, bus number 283 goes right to the centre (some of the vehicles have a duck logo or poster). www.wwt.org.uk

Below: *Walpole House at Chiswick.*

CHISWICK

Its pleasant riverside location makes the 'village' of Chiswick a good finishing point for a walk along the banks of the Thames, with the attractive **Chiswick Mall** boasting a series of grand houses overlooking the houseboats moored on the tidal reaches. The atmospheric **Church Lane** was the original medieval high street, with the graveyard of the church of **St Nicholas** (which has a 15th-century tower) containing the graves of painters JM Whistler and William Hogarth. **Hogarth's House** is just a short stroll away, with many of his famous satirical engravings – which so enraged the establishment at the time – displayed inside. Open 13:00–17:00 Tue–Fri (16:00 Nov–Mar); 13:00–18:00 Sat–Sun and holiday Mon (–17:00 Nov–Mar).

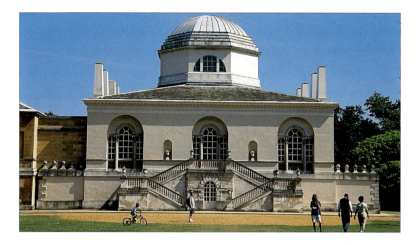

Chiswick House ★★

The highlight of Chiswick is Chiswick House, a classical, Palladian-style villa built by Lord Burlington in 1729. It was designed as a gallery for his art collection and as a setting for meeting his coterie, which included Alexander Pope, Jonathan Swift, and composers such as Handel. Inside the house is a domed octagonal hall, where paintings and sculptures were once displayed. Don't miss the sumptuously redecorated Blue Velvet Room or the noted Chiswick Tables (in the gallery). The house is surrounded by superb gardens, complete with Roman statuary and an Ionic temple overlooking a grassy amphitheatre with a pond. Open Apr–Oct only: 10:00–17:00 Wed–Sun and holiday Mon (closing 14:00 Sat). www.english-heritage.org.uk

Kew Bridge Steam Museum ★

This old Victorian water works, at Green Dragon Lane, Brentford, features a massive Steam Hall with four monster Cornish beam engines, maintained by volunteers and fired up at weekends and holiday Mon: the best time to visit if you're a steam enthusiast. There's also a miniature steam railway and displays on the history of water power. Open 11:00–17:00 Tue–Sun. www.kbsm.org

Above: *Built around a central octagonal room, Chiswick House is a classic example of Palladian-style architecture.*

Below: *Chiswick Mall and Church, seen from the Thames.*

Right: *Osterley House, a fine example of neo-classical Robert Adam architecture.*
Opposite: *Victoria Regis water lilies in the Princess of Wales Conservatory at Kew Gardens.*

SYON AND OSTERLEY
Syon House ★★

Renovated by designer Robert Adam in the late 1700s, **Syon House** contains some exuberant period interiors, notably the ornate Ante Room, splendid Red Drawing Room and elegant Long Gallery. House open 11:00–16:15 Wed, Thu, Sun and holiday Mon, Mar/Apr–Oct. The lovely 200-acre **park**, landscaped by Capability Brown, opens daily throughout the year 10:00–17:30/dusk. www.syonpark.co.uk

Butterflies

The delightful London Butterfly House is being forced to move from Syon. At the time of going to press, it is hoping to obtain financing to move to Crystal Palace. www.butterflies.org.uk

Osterley House and Park ★

One of the last great country houses with an intact estate within the London area, Osterley House is approached through the park along an avenue of towering chestnut trees, and past an ornamental lake with a pagoda. The neoclassical house is one of the finest remaining examples of the work of Robert Adam and has richly decorated interiors. The house is open 13:00–16:30, Wed–Sun and holiday Mon, Easter–Oct. The Park is open year-round from 09:00 to sunset daily. www.osterleypark.org.uk

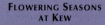

FLOWERING SEASONS AT KEW

- **January:** Camellias, shrubs, alpines and heathers.
- **February:** Orchids and snowdrops.
- **March:** Daffodils, crocuses and cherry blossom.
- **April:** Magnolias, tulips and spring bedding.
- **May:** Bluebells, azaleas and lilac.
- **June:** Roses, rhododendrons and chestnut trees.
- **July & August:** Giant waterlilies, summer bedding and scented plants.
- **September:** Summer bulbs and start of autumn colour.
- **October:** Late-flowering crocuses and cyclamens.
- **November:** The last of the autumn foliage.
- **December:** Strawberry trees, holly – and Christmas lights.

KEW
Kew Gardens ★★★

Covering 121ha (300 acres) on the banks of the Thames, the Royal Botanic Gardens is a fascinating place to visit. It houses the world's greatest collections of plants and plant material, and is a major research centre for the economic and medicinal uses of plants, some of which have become extinct in their original habitats; many others are endangered. Kew Gardens also boasts four of the largest glasshouses in the world and it was awarded UNESCO World Heritage Site status in 2003.

The main entrance (open daily 09:30–dusk) is Victoria Gate, Lichfield Road; pick up a (free) map there. Almost opposite is the **Palm House**, a masterpiece of Victorian engineering in iron and glass. To the east is the **Princess of Wales Conservatory**, Kew's most humid environment, noted for giant waterlilies and other tropical plants. To the west of the Palm House is the elegant **Temperate House**, the largest of Kew's glasshouses and a superb setting for many exotic species, citrus fruits, and the world's largest indoor plant (the Chilean Wine Palm: over 16m high). The **Evolution House**, behind it, traces the development of plant life on the planet over the last 3500 million years.

Other highlights – of which there are many – include a **Pagoda**, the **Marianne North Gallery** (housing botanical paintings) and **Queen Charlotte's Cottage** (once a royal summer house). The smallest royal residence in the country is the intimate **Kew Palace**, tucked away on the north side of the gardens; George III and Queen Charlotte used it as their family retreat from 1802–1818 and it was subsequently the place where the king was confined during his increasingly-frequent attacks of porphyria – which was wrongly diagnosed as madness. www.rbgkew.org.uk

KEW PALACE

Newly opened to the public, after a £6.6 million restoration project, Kew Palace cleverly uses audio tapes in the form of conversations between various members of the royal family to evoke the presence of its former occupants.

The ground floor has a bust of George III created by Madame Tussaud herself, artefacts related to his interests and a Baby House decorated by the princesses. The first floor has been recreated as faithfully as possible to look as opulent as it did in his reign. The top floor is in a state of disrepair with fragments of the original décor still visible.

Right: *A view of the Thames from Richmond. Easily accessible from Richmond, with its famous park, beautiful buildings and riverside location, has a lot to offer.* **Opposite:** *Riverboats at Hampton Court.*

RICHMOND

This riverside town's main attraction is its enormous Park (see below), but there are other sights nearby which are of interest. Between the modern high street and the Thames lies **Richmond Green**, a lovely square surrounded by Queen Anne and Georgian houses. On the southwest corner a Tudor gateway is all that remains of **Richmond Palace**, dating back to the 12th century but extensively rebuilt by the Tudors. A famous view, embracing the Thames Valley and no less than six counties, is the main reward for climbing **Richmond Hill**, behind the town.

Richmond Park ★★

Beyond Richmond Hill stretches the huge expanse of Richmond Park, created by Charles I who hunted here and enclosed it within a 16km (10 mile) long wall (still there today) in the 17th century. At 1000ha (2471 acres) it is easily the largest city park in Europe, and features rolling grasslands interspersed with coppices, woodland (mostly oak, beech and chestnut) and ponds. Much of this is natural wilderness, apart from the landscaped plantations of rhododendron and azaleas, which provide gorgeous displays in the spring. Sizeable herds of red and fallow deer roam all over the park, and twitchers will also find plenty of birdlife (particularly in **Sidmouth Wood**, which is a bird sanctuary).

HAMPTON COURT PALACE

Set in 24ha (59 acres) of landscaped gardens and parklands adjoining the River Thames (the annual Flower Show is a major event), Hampton Court is probably the most dazzling of all the royal palaces in England. Don't forget to try the renowned maze.

Of all the monarchs who have lived here it is most closely associated with Henry VIII, and today the tapestry of court life in Tudor times is vividly brought to life by costumed actors leading tours through this rambling, turreted building. Self-guided audio tours are also available.

Entering the **palace** you find yourself in Base Court, which leads to Clock Court and then on to Fountain Court, all of which are surrounded by royal apartments. The Great Hall of **Henry VIII's State Apartments** has an ornate double-hammerbeam roof – Shakespeare's theatrical players performed here under Elizabeth I. Other major rooms are the Great Watching Chamber, the Haunted Gallery, and the Royal Chapel. The **Queen's Apartments** are largely 18th century, as are the **Georgian Rooms**. Within the **King's Apartments** (built for William III), don't miss the elaborate display of weapons in the King's Guard Chamber. The prodigious consumption of the Royal Court is vividly brought to life in the massive **Tudor Kitchens**, which have been restored to show preparations for a feast day in 1542.

Open daily 10:00–17:00 Apr–Oct; 10:00–15:30 Nov–Mar. www.hrp.org.uk

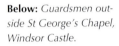

Windsor Area

WINDSOR

Below: *Guardsmen outside St George's Chapel, Windsor Castle.*

The network of cobbled streets of Windsor's Old Town is filled with antique and souvenir shops and features several interesting buildings, including **Burford House** (where

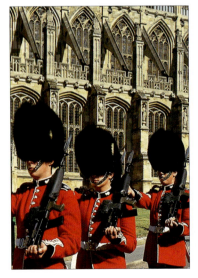

Charles II housed his mistress Nell Gwynne), and the **Guildhall,** standing on pillars in the High Street, which was completed by Sir Christopher Wren.

Windsor Castle ★★★

The oldest and largest inhabited castle in England and the official weekend residence of the Queen, Windsor Castle's imposing battlements and turrets dominate the town from its hilltop site, 40km (25 miles) from central London.

Originally a timber and earth stronghold built by William the Conqueror, the castle steadily grew in importance during Norman and Plantagenet times and was rebuilt in stone by Henry II. The present design was influenced by George III and George IV: it was the latter who added a bigger **Round**

Tower – one of the castle's most distinguishing features – and many of the state apartments.

Entering the castle you go through the Middle Ward, with the Round Tower in its centre. Continue past the Winchester Gates to the North Terrace, where there are superb views over the Chiltern Hills and Eton College. Here is the entrance to the **State Apartments**, badly damaged in a major fire in 1992 but now fully restored to their former splendour. Amid the gilded ceilings and ornate furnishings are several important works by Rubens, Rembrandt and Van Dyck as well as superb Gobelin tapestries. Don't miss the exquisite **Queen Mary's Dolls House**, an extraordinary creation which took three years to complete. Designed by Edwin Lutyens in 1920, the house has working plumbing, lifts, and electricity. The **Drawings Gallery** features themed exhibitions from the extensive Royal Collection of paintings, sculpture and objets d'art. Usually open daily 09:45–15:00/16:00, but can vary, so check. Tel: (01753) 831 118. www.royalcollection.org.uk

Passing through the Lower Ward you reach **St George's Chapel**, one of the finest ecclesiastical buildings in England, begun in 1475 by Edward IV. Ten monarchs (including Henry VIII and his favourite wife, Jane Seymour) are buried here; one of the best times to visit is when the choir is singing evensong (17:15 daily).

Eton ★

A short walk takes you from Windsor to Eton, home of one of Britain's most famous 'public' schools, where pupils wear a characteristic uniform of top hat and morning coat. Over the years, Eton has educated many of the country's prime ministers and top politicians.

GETTING THERE

Windsor is around 50 minutes by train from central London, with frequent services from Waterloo to Windsor & Eton Riverside and from Paddington to Windsor Central (change at Slough). Both stations are close to the town centre. Green Line coaches operate daily from Victoria, tel: (0870) 608 7261. www.greenline.co.uk For details on train times or other information contact the Information Centre, 24 High Street, tel: (01753) 743 900. Open daily 10:00–17:30 in summer; 10:00–17:00 in spring and autumn; 10:00–16:00 in winter.

Overleaf: *Looking across the Millennium Bridge at St Paul's Cathedral from the South Bank.*

Below: *Windsor Castle viewed from the Long Walk.*

London at a Glance

London's unpredictable weather (see p. 6–7) means that it is always best to pack rainwear. The climate is essentially temperate, however, and there are sunny days throughout the year.
The city is least crowded Oct–Easter and busiest Jul–Aug. Book summer accommodation well in advance.

GETTING THERE

By Air: There are direct flights to the UK from all major cities. The main airports for international flights are **Heathrow**, **Gatwick** and **Stansted**. All the airport transfers detailed below operate from about 05:00 until midnight, so you should have no problem making flight connections.
• **Heathrow:** 24km (14 miles) west of central London. The fastest way to the city centre is by **Heathrow Express** into Paddington, which takes 15 mins (23 mins for Terminal 4) and runs every 15 mins. The **Piccadilly Underground Line** is cheaper, takes an hour and runs every 5 to 10 mins, but there's no dedicated space for baggage. **Taxis** from Heathrow are generally expensive (allow £40–50).
• **Gatwick:** 50km (30 miles) south of London. The **Gatwick Express** runs from the airport to Victoria Station, taking 30 mins, and operating every 15 mins – every 30 mins early morning and late evening.

• **Stansted:** 60km (37 miles) northeast is London's third airport. **Stansted Express** runs to Liverpool Street station every 15–30 minutes and takes about 45 minutes. Coaches are cheaper, but take twice as long.
• **London City Airport:** In London Docklands, mostly used by commuters to and from Paris, Brussels, Amsterdam and other European cities. **Blue shuttle bus** to Liverpool Street station (taking 30 mins) every 10–15 mins – every 25 mins at weekends; or to connect with the **Docklands Light Railway (DLR)**, Canary Wharf.

By Road and Sea: Visitors from Europe may choose **ferry services** from the Channel ports or the **Channel Tunnel**. Services through the tunnel include **Le Shuttle** for drivers and **Eurostar** trains for passengers, running direct from Paris and Brussels with connecting services from other European departure points.

GETTING AROUND

London has an extensive public transport system: an efficient **bus system**, **black taxis**, and the **Underground** trains (the 'tube'). Congested streets mean that the tube remains the quickest and most practical mode of travel. Transport for London (TfL) discourage the use of single tickets by constantly raising

prices, so get a pass. Tubes and buses are zoned, Zone 1 being the central (and most expensive) of the 6 areas, and your pass must cover all zones travelled. Visitor passes can be obtained before reaching London, so visit your travel agent or www.tfl.gov.uk. Once in London, you can get information and free transport maps (inc. river services) from all TICs (travel or tourist information centres), most tube stations or National Rail stations and many newsagents. Bus passes are the cheapest but if you intend to use the tube or DLR (Docklands Light Railway) as well, you will need a Travelcard or Oyster card.
The Tube (Underground): There are 12 lines, covering most districts but sparse south of the Thames.
Trains run 05:00–00:30 (07:30–23:30 Sun).
Buses: Most buses run 04:30–24:00, **night buses** (N prefix before the route number) run 24:00–04:30 and daily passes expire at 04:30. Many drivers stop only if hailed from a bus-stop – or if you ring the bell to get off – so treat all stops as if they were request stops.
Taxis: London's famous **black cabs** (nowadays often coloured or covered in sponsors' adverts) run on meters according to the distance travelled and time of day. Taxis can be hailed on the street (when the yellow TAXI

London at a Glance

sign is lit, it means they are available). To summon a **black cab** by phone, tel: (0871) 871 8710, but be warned: you'll pay *at least* £2 more than if you signal one that's cruising. Licensed **minicabs** are usually cheaper (agree a price before setting off) and *must* be summoned by phone. **NEVER** get into one that is touting for business on the street: such 'cabs' are operated illegally and are notoriously dangerous, particularly for lone women.

The West End
LUXURY

Brown's Hotel, 30–34 Albemarle Street, W1, tel: (020) 7493 6020. Popular, old-fashioned; furnished with antiques.

Claridge's, Brook Street, W1, tel: (020) 7629 8860. Favourite with royalty and superstars. It's expensive, but service is good.

The Dorchester, 53 Park Lane, W1, tel: (020) 7629 8888. One of London's landmark hotels, overlooking Hyde Park, popular with movie stars.

The London Hilton, 22 Park Lane, W1, tel: (0800) 282 493. Excellent views of Hyde Park; impeccable service and décor.

The Ritz, 150 Piccadilly, W1 tel: (020) 7493 8181. Steeped in history and an attraction in its own right, it has opulent Louis XVI décor with the

west-facing rooms (facing Green Park) the best ones to book.

MID-RANGE

The Goring, 15 Beeston Place, SW1, tel: (020) 7396 9000. Well-located, family-run hotel with elegant public rooms and spacious *en-suite* bedrooms.

Hazlitt's, 6 Frith Street, W1, tel: (020) 7434 1771. Period-style rooms in 18th-century home of essayist William Hazlitt.

Bloomsbury and Covent Garden
LUXURY

The Savoy, Strand, WC2, tel: (020) 7836 4343. Synonymous with top service and luxury; spacious rooms decorated in Art Deco. Good fitness centre.

MID-RANGE

Radisson Edwardian Mountbatten, 20 Monmouth St, WC2, tel: (020) 7836 4300. Country-house-style hotel in Covent Garden, with Lord Mountbatten memorabilia.

BUDGET

Ruskin, 23–24 Montague Street, WC1, tel: (020) 7636 7388. Excellent location in Bloomsbury, good value.

West and Southwest London
LUXURY

The Beaufort, 33 Beaufort Gardens, SW3, tel: (020)

7584 5252. Stylish hotel with large, modern rooms and good value for money.

Blakes, 33 Roland Gardens, SW7, tel: (020) 7370 6701. Popular with celebrities. Glamorous interiors and suites.

MID-RANGE

The Gallery Hotel, 8–10 Queensberry Place, SW7, tel: (020) 7915 0000. Traditional Georgian with spacious suites.

The Pelham, 15 Cromwell Place, SW7, tel: (020) 7589 8288. Small, comfortable; with individually decorated rooms.

BUDGET

Amsterdam Hotel, 7 Trebovir Road, SW5. Tel: (020) 7370 5084. Comfortable B&B near Earl's Court, all rooms with en-suite facilities.

Gower Hotel, 129 Sussex Gardens, W2, tel: (020) 7262 2262. Family-run hotel in conveniently located listed building, all rooms en suite.

Hotel 167, 167 Old Brompton Rd, SW5, tel: (020) 7373 0672. Slightly upmarket B&B, all rooms with en suite facilities.

The City, the East End and Docklands
MID-RANGE

Thistle Barbican Hotel, 120 Central St, EC1, tel: (020) 7251 1565. Modern hotel, close to Barbican Arts Centre and City.

London at a Glance

Thistle Tower Hotel, St Katherine's Way, E1, tel: (0870) 333 9106. Modern; superbly situated next to Tower Bridge.

North London
BUDGET
Kandara Guest House, 68 Ockenden Road, N1, tel: (020) 7226 5721. Small family-run establishment with 12 bedrooms and 6 shared bathrooms.

Further Afield
MID-RANGE
Petersham Hotel, Nightingale Lane, Richmond tel: (020) 8940 7471. Near Richmond Park; views over the Thames.
The Windmill, Clapham Common Southside, tel: (020) 8673 4578. On the edge of Clapham Common, with few competitors; reasonable value.

In addition to the ubiquitous fast-food places, London has several good-quality chains with reasonable prices and branches in strategic locations. So look out for: **Café Rouge** (French), **PRÊT À MANGER** (chemical-free sandwiches and other snacks), **SUBWAY** (interesting sandwiches made to order), **Bella Pasta** (Italian), **Café Flo** (French), **Garfunkel's** (American), **Sofra** (Turkish), **Café Uno** (Italian), **Cork & Bottle**

(wine-bars with good food), **Micky's** (proper traditional fish and chips). Many of the **cafés in galleries and museums** are excellent.

Whitehall and Westminster
Tate Britain Restaurant, Tate Britain, Millbank, SW1, tel: (020) 7887 8000. Spacious, imposing setting, with changing menu and excellent desserts.

The West End
Aperitivo, 41 Beak St, W1, tel: (020) 7287 2057. The Italian version of tapas.
Tokyo Diner, 2 Newport Place, WC2, tel: (020) 7287 8777. Limited but excellent Japanese food at affordable prices.
Gay Hussar, 2 Greek Street, W1, tel: (020) 7437 0973. Famous and long-established Hungarian restaurant.
Hard Rock Café, 150 Old Park Lane, W1, tel: (020) 7514 1700. The place for real burgers – at a price. Be prepared to queue.
Sports Café, 80 Haymarket, SW1, tel: (020) 7839 8300. Countless satellite channels on over 100 TVs; restaurant, 4 bars and a dance floor.
The Stockpot, 38 Panton Street, London WC2, tel: (020) 7839 5142. Possibly the cheapest filling meal in town.
Kettners, 29 Romilly Street, W1, tel: (020) 7734 6112. Trendy and in an interesting old building.

Bloomsbury and Covent Garden
Simpson's in the Strand, 100 Strand, WC2, tel: (020) 7836 9112. Very traditional; waiters wheeling out silver platters of beef and the like. Excellent puddings and breakfasts.
Porters English Restaurant, 17 Henrietta Street, WC2, tel: (020) 7836 6466. Long-established source of fine fare.
Sarastro (see p. 28), 126 Drury Lane, WC2, tel: (020) 7836 0101, and **Papageno**, 29–31 Wellington Street, WC2, tel: (020) 7836 4444. Late opening (serving until 23:45), Mediterranean cuisine (especially fish) in operatic décor.

West and Southwest London
Bibendum, Michelin House, 81 Fulham Rd, SW3, tel: (020) 7581 5817. Classy, eclectic cuisine in delightful old Michelin building. Pricey, but worth it.
Chutney Mary, 535 King's Rd, SW10, tel: (020) 7351 3113. Best of 'British Raj' cooking and regional Indian dishes.
La Gavroche, 43 Upper Brook Street, W1, tel: (020) 7408 0881. One of the world's top 50 restaurants, famous for the high standard of its classic French cuisine.
Kam Tong, 59–63 Queensway, W2, tel: (020) 7229 6065. Popular, with excellent Cantonese food – in an area offering many other good eating options.

London at a Glance

North London

Belgo Noord, 72 Chalk Farm Road, NW1, tel: (020) 7267 0718. Amusing décor; inexpensive and generous portions of Belgian favourites; but book in advance.

Sea Shell, 49–51 Lisson Grove, NW1, tel: (020) 7224 9000. Arguably the best fish-and-chippie in town.

South and Southeast London

Butler's Wharf Chop House, Butler's Wharf, 36E Shad Thames, SE1, tel: (020) 7403 3403. Fabulous views of Tower Bridge from Terence Conran's riverfront restaurant. Traditional British food at its best.

Le Pont de la Tour, Butler's Wharf, 36D Shad Thames, SE1, tel: (020) 7403 8403. Another Conran outpost, overlooking the river. Attentive service, exhaustive wine list, accent on seafoods.

WHERE TO SHOP

Napoleon dubbed the English a 'nation of shopkeepers' and London has something for everyone, whatever your tastes or your budget, from grand department stores to speciality shops or bargain-basement market stalls.

Opening hours vary – mostly 09:00/10:00–17:30/19:00 Monday–Saturday, noon to 16:00/18:00 Sunday. On holiday Mondays most shops open – but only for Sunday hours. Many of the earlier-closing shops have one night a week on which they stay open until around 20:00. Many shops are also open longer hours in the month before Christmas.

Prices are considerably reduced during the two major **sales** periods, with the winter sales – the biggest event – running from around Christmas until early February, and the summer sales starting in June or July. All the large shops (and most of the smaller ones) accept **credit cards**, as do most other establishments, but **traveller's cheques** are not commonly accepted as a form of payment.

Overseas visitors can sometimes claim back **sales tax** (VAT, or Value Added Tax) on goods purchased (*see* **Money Matters**, p. 122). London has tens of thousands of shops, so it would take a whole book to list them all; this rundown covers some of the main shopping areas.

Oxford Street and Surrounds

Almost a mile long, **Oxford Street** may be one of the most famous shopping streets in the capital but the stretch to the east of Oxford Circus is rather tawdry, filled with tacky souvenir shops and second-rate cut-price clothing. It is the stretch west of Oxford Circus that contains most of the more upmarket establishments and is home to major chains and department stores such as Selfridges, Marks & Spencer, John Lewis, Next, Debenhams, GAP and adidas, as well as outlets for such companies as HMV, Disney and Laura Ashley. To the north of Oxford Street, **St Christopher's Place** features numerous designer outlets, whilst on the opposite side **South Molton Street** is another popular area for fashion boutiques. Leading off Oxford Street, **Bond Street** and **New Bond Street** feature quality fashions, haute couture, art galleries, jewellery and antique shops. Leading down from Oxford Circus to Piccadilly, **Regent Street** is home to Liberty's department store, habitat, Hamleys toyshop, Levi's, the Apple Store, several crystal and china shops, jewellery stores and classic British clothing shops such as Aquascutum, Jaeger and Austin Reed. To the east of Regent Street, **Carnaby Street** was world famous during the 'Swinging Sixties' and is becoming trendy again, with name stores and such interesting alternative shops as Lush (handmade soap and the like).

Running parallel to Regent Street on its west side, **Savile Row** is well known as the best place to go for bespoke tailoring.

London at a Glance

Piccadilly and St James's
Piccadilly Circus features the indoor shopping complexes of the Trocadero, as well as Virgin and Lillywhites, the sports department store. **Piccadilly** has an eclectic mix of stores, including such famous names as Fortnum and Mason (food), De Beers (diamonds) and Hatchards (books). South of Piccadilly in St James's is **Jermyn Street**, which has numerous small, old-fashioned shops offering exciting finds such as beautiful hand-made shoes, shirts and the like.
On the north side of Piccadilly, the **Burlington Arcade** is another old-fashioned enclave with good quality shops selling everything from porcelain to antique jewellery, Irish linen and cashmere jumpers.

Knightsbridge, Kensington and Chelsea
One of the most expensive shopping areas in the capital, **Knightsbridge** features numerous classy boutiques and designer fashion shops, as well as world-famous Harrods. **Sloane Street**, with Harvey Nichols and yet more expensive clothing outlets, leads down into **Sloane Square** and the beginning of **King's Road**. Once one of London's great fashion meccas, King's Road can still hold its own, with a lot of trendy designer outlets.

Kensington has antique shops along **Kensington Church Street**, department stores and clothes boutiques on **Kensington High Street**, and also a cluster of British-based design outlets, with superb windows, situated in Beauchamp Place.
Covent Garden and Soho
Covent Garden has a wonderfully eclectic mix of shops, selling virtually everything from designer clothes to arts, crafts, books, antiques and more. To the north of Covent Garden, **Floral Street** is hot on street fashions, while **Neal's Yard** tends to be the focus for rather 'alternative' goods and wholefoods.
Alongside the pornographic outlets in **Soho** there are many unusual specialist shops, from Continental delicatessens to small record outlets.
Between Soho and Covent Garden, **Charing Cross Road** is synonymous with the book trade, with numerous specialized outlets (for both new and secondhand books), and major bookstores such as the renowned Foyle (No. 119).

MARKETS

London has a vast range of markets, rewarding places to browse for crafts, antiques, and bargains of every description among the hordes. Some of the better known ones include
Brick Lane near Spitalfields

(Sun 06:00–14:00)
Petticoat Lane Middlesex Street (clothes, bric-a-brac and spiel: best Sun 09:00–14:00); www.eastlondonmarkets.com
Portobello Road (general: Mon–Wed 08:00–18:00), Thu 09:00–13:00, Fri–Sat 07:00–19:00, but antiques: Sat 06:00–18:00;
Greenwich (bric-a-brac, arts, crafts, clothes: 09:30–17:00 Thu–Sun) and the **Camden** markets (*see* p. 86).

DEPARTMENT STORES

Fortnum and Mason, 181 Piccadilly, W1, tel: (020) 7734 8040. Open 10:00–18:30 Mon–Sat. Food Hall also opens Sun 12:00–18:00.
Harrods, 87 Brompton Road, SW1, tel: (020) 7730 1234. Open 10:00–20:00, Mon–Sat, 12:00–18:00 Sun.
Harvey Nichols, 102–125 Knightsbridge, SW1, tel: (020) 7235 5000. Open 10:00–20:00 Mon–Sat, 12:00–18:00 Sun.
John Lewis, 278–306 Oxford Street, W1, tel: (020) 7629 7711. Open 09:30–19:00 Mon–Wed and Fri–Sat, 10:00–20:00 Thu, 12:00–18:00 Sun.
Liberty, 212–299 Regent Street, W1, tel: (020) 7734 1234. Open 10:00–19:00 Mon–Sat, 10:00–20:00 Thu, 12:00–18:00 Sun.
Marks & Spencer (their flagship store), 458 Oxford Street, W1, tel: (020) 7935

7954. Open 09:00–21:00 Mon–Fri, 09:00–20:00 Sat, 12:00–18:00 Sun.
Selfridges, 400 Oxford Street, W1, tel: (0870) 837 7377. Open 09:00–20:00 Mon–Wed and Fri, 09:30–21:00 Thu, 09:30–20:00 Sat, 12:00–18:00 Sun.

TOURS AND EXCURSIONS

One of the greatest advantages of visiting London is that there are so many other interesting places within a reasonable distance of the capital which you can visit for an enjoyable day out, or even for a slightly longer stay. With frequent train services from the eight main rail termini in central London you don't have to worry about driving either; coaches are another option, with hundreds of services from the Victoria Coach Station daily. **Victoria Coach Station**, 164 Buckingham Palace Road, SW1. The following tour operators offer day-tours from London to all the major tourist destinations, and all use qualified Blue Badge Guides:
Golden Tours,
(020) 7233 7030.
Evan Evans,
(020) 7950 1777.
Frames Rickards,
(020) 7828 9720.
Hallam Anderson Tours,
(020) 7436 9304.
To the southeast of London, **Canterbury** has long been a place of pilgrimage, with the

focal point being the city's magnificent cathedral. The vibrant Sussex coastal town of **Brighton** has a distinguished Regency heritage, excellent shopping and a traditional English seaside pier; the highlight is the refurbished Royal Pavilion, the seaside palace of George IV. The coastline of Central Southern England features numerous popular seaside resorts as well as the historic naval port of **Portsmouth**. Further inland are the ancient cathedral cities of **Winchester** and **Salisbury**. Near Salisbury, the monoliths of **Stonehenge** are one of the country's most famous prehistoric monuments. The West Country features numerous picturesque villages, stately homes and historic monuments. In the county of Avon, **Bath** was first popularized by the Romans as a spa town and with its fine Georgian architecture considered one of the most elegant towns in the country (it has good shops, too). To the north of Bath, the **Cotswolds** are famous for their pretty, honey-coloured sandstone villages set amongst rolling hills. One of the finest medieval castles in the country is to be found at **Warwick**, to the north of the Cotswolds, while nearby **Stratford-upon-Avon** is, of course, the much-visited birthplace of the father of

theatre, William Shakespeare. Central England is home to the ancient university town of **Oxford**, where many of the graceful college buildings are open to the public. Further east, the rival university town of **Cambridge** also boasts many fine buildings which can be explored by punt along the river or on foot.

USEFUL CONTACTS

VisitLondon: can be contacted during office hours, tel: (0870) 156 6366 or visit www.visitlondon.com or www.londontown.com.
Disabled: VisitLondon's site has a section with information of all kinds for the disabled: select Accessible London. The TfL Customer Services line can advise about transport, tel: (0845) 300 7000. For entertainment, try Artsline, tel: (020) 7388 2227. Dial UK can provide other information of use to the disabled, tel: (01302) 310 123.
Transport for London (TfL): enquiry service for buses, tubes, DLR and river boats, tel: (020) 7222 1234 (manned 24/7).
Docklands Light Railway (DLR): tel: (020) 7363 9700.
National Train Enquiries: tel: (08457) 48 49 50. www.nationalrail.co.uk
National Express (coach service): tel: (0870) 575 7747. www.nationalexpress.com
Victoria Coach Station: tel: (020) 7730 3466.

London at a Glance

Public Carriage Office (complaints and licensing queries): tel: (0845) 602 7000.
Lost Property: Mon–Fri 08:30–16:00, tel: (020) 7918 2000 or (0845) 330 9882.
Heathrow Airport: tel: (0870) 000 0123. www.baa.co.uk
Gatwick Airport: tel: (0870) 000 2468. www.baa.co.uk
London City Airport: tel: (020) 7646 0088. www.londoncityairport.com
Stansted Airport: tel: (0870) 000 0303. www.baa.co.uk

Car Rental:
Avis: tel: (0870) 010 0287. www.avis.co.uk
Hertz: tel: (020) 7730 8323. www.hertz.co.uk
Easycar: tel: (0906) 333 3333. www.easycar.com

Double-decker hop-on hop-off sightseeing tours
These are an excellent introduction to London, providing masses of background information and a variety of special offers, including tickets for some attractions that enable you to queue-jump. Tickets are valid for 24 hours and you can get on and off at any stop. The two main companies have frequent services and stops that are convenient for the sights. Most vehicles have open top decks.
Big Bus, tel: (020) 7233 9533; www.bigbustours.com
The Original Tour, tel: (020) 8877 1722; www.theoriginaltour.com

Driver Guides:
• Flexible itineraries are tailored to your interests and personalized service are among the advantages of a driver-guided tour.
• **Black Taxi Tours of London**, tel: (020) 7935 9363.
• **British Tours**, tel: (020) 7734 8734.
• **Take a Guide**, tel: (020) 8960 0459.

Guide Booking Agencies:
The London registered guides have all undertaken a rigorous training course, after which they are issued with the coveted Blue Badge and photocard licence. The companies listed below can book Blue Badge guides for anything from general sightseeing to special interest tours:
• **Professional Guide Services**, tel: (020) 8874 2745.
• **Tours Guides International**, tel: (020) 7495 5504.

Walking and Cycling Tours:
There are several outfits offering walks, so consult listings and the tourist websites (see above). The oldest is **Original London Walks**, which offers 40 or so walks with different themes, tel: (020) 7624 3978. www.walks.com.
Alternatively, **The London Bicycle Tour Co.**, Gabriels Wharf, offers several guided weekend rides – mainly in East London. Tel: (020) 7928 6838. www.londonbicycle.com

River Boat Operators:
For full details, pick up a river services booklet (see p. 115).
Turks Launches (upriver from Westminster to Hampton Court, via Kew and Richmond): tel: (020) 8546 2434. www.turks.co.uk
NB: Travelcards are not valid.
Catamaran Cruisers (between Embankment and Greenwich, with hop-on, hop-off Hopper fare; also multi-lingual circular cruise from Westminster): tel: (020) 7987 1185. www.catamarancruisers.co.uk
Thames River Services (between Westminster and Greenwich, some continuing to the Thames Barrier): tel: (020) 7930 4097.
City Cruises (hop-on, hop-off with Red Rover day ticket between Westminster and Greenwich; also **London Showboat**, a cabaret and dinner cruise from Westminster): tel: (020) 7740 0400.
Crown River Cruises (hop-on, hop-off circular route between Westminster and St Katherine's): tel: (020) 7936 2033. www.crownriver.com
Bateaux London (jazz, lunch and dinner cruises from Embankment and Waterloo): tel: (020) 7925 2215. www.bateauxlondon.com

Canal Boats:
Jason's Canal Boat, tel: (020) 7286 3428.
London Waterbus, tel: (020) 7482 2550, or 24-hour recording (020) 7482 2660.

Travel Tips

Tourist Information

Overseas offices of **VisitBritish** have a range of leaflets, brochures, free maps and guides, and events calendars. Offices can be found in Australia (Sydney), Canada (Toronto), Ireland (Dublin), New Zealand (Auckland), South Africa (Sandton), Singapore, and the USA (New York); www.visitbritain.com The main tourist office in London is the **British Visitor Centre**, 1 Lower Regent Street, SW1, open Mon 09:30–18:30, Tue–Fri 09:00–18:30 and Sun 10:00–16:00 all year; Sat 09:00–17:00 June–Sep, 10:00–16:00 Oct–May, tel: (0870) 156 6366, www.visitlondon.com. Another informative site is www.londontown.com – a comprehensive site with a free booking service.

There is an official tourist information centre (TIC) in the Arrivals Hall of the International Terminal at Waterloo station, open daily 08:30–22:00, tel: (020) 7620 1550. There are also (un-official desks/offices at some airports and mainline stations,

but their information is usually limited.

There are a few official local TICs which provide comprehensive information about their areas, notably City (see p. 73), Southwark (see p. 99), Greenwich (see p. 102), and Richmond (see p. 110).

Entry Requirements

No visas are required by citizens of the USA, Canada, Australia, New Zealand, Japan, Norway, Iceland, Switzerland and the European Union (EU). Many other Commonwealth citizens are also exempt, but should check, as should nationals of all other countries. www.ukvisas.gov.uk

Customs

For goods bought outside the EU, these restrictions on tax- and duty-free goods apply:
• 200 cigarettes, or 100 cigarillos, or 50 cigars, or 250g (8 ounces) tobacco.
• 2 litres (4 pints) still table wine plus 1 litre (2 pints) spirits or liqueur (over 22% proof), or 2 litres (4 pints) of fortified or sparkling wine

(under 22% proof).
• 60ml (2 fluid ounces) perfume plus 250ml (8 fluid ounces) of toilet water.
• Other goods valued to £145.
Restrictions apply on the import of other items (firearms, protected species, meat products, etc) and pets. There are no restrictions on currency.

Health Requirements

No vaccinations are required.

Money Matters

Currency: British currency is the pound sterling (£), divided into 100 pence (p). Coin denominations are 1p, 2p, 5p, 10p, 20p, 50p, £1 and £2. Notes are in denominations of £5, £10, £20, £50.
Banks: The four major banks, with branches throughout the city are: National Westminster, Barclays, Lloyds and HSBC. Standard opening hours are 09:30–17:00, Mon–Fri, but there are variations. Some branches open for a few hours on Sat.
Currency Exchange: Traveller's cheques: You'll need your passport when

cashing traveller's cheques. Commission is usually charged. Banks offer the best rates, but numerous **bureaux de change** work longer hours.
Credit cards: Most hotels, shops and restaurants accept international credit cards.
VAT: Consumer goods (with major exceptions such as food and books) are subject to a 17.5% sales tax known as VAT (Value Added Tax). Visitors from non-EU countries can recoup VAT on major items but, before you buy, ask for the appropriate form. Customs will validate this when you leave.
Tipping: Service charges are usually included in bills, but many restaurants leave a blank space on credit card counterfoils to encourage customers to tip twice! If a tip is not included, waiters expect 10–15%. Hairdressers and taxis expect a tip of about 10%. If there's a saucer in well-maintained washrooms, add a coin or two. Don't tip if service has been poor. Bar staff (but not in pubs) may also expect a tip.

Accommodation
London has many options, ranging from the **deluxe** to homely **bed and breakfasts** (B&Bs), **hostels** and **budget hotels**. Even in peak season there is rarely a shortage of places to stay but London is an expensive city, and this is more than reflected in the price of hotel rooms.
Accommodation agencies: **VisitLondon** have over 1000 hotels and other accommo-

dation of all types on their books within a 20km radius of the capital. Free reservations by credit card, tel: (020) 7234 5800, Mon–Fri 09:00–17:30, or go to www.visitlondon.com. You can also get help from the British Visitor Centre or any TIC (*see* p. 122). Another free service is on www.londontown.com, with discounts and a search facility. Tel: (020) 7437 4370 or (0800) 566 366.
British Hotels Reservation Centres (BHRC) have branches at Heathrow, Gatwick and Stansted airports, Victoria, Paddington and Waterloo rail stations and Victoria coach station. Bookings are free; tel: (0845) 604 4060 or (0800) 282 888.
Hotels and B&Bs: Hotels are classified by stars and all other types of accommodation by diamonds (both 1–5), with ratings depending on quality and range of facilities. These determine categories but give no indication of

character or style. Establishments with 4 or more rooms are required to display notices of charges, and whether this includes breakfast, service charges, VAT, etc.
In the off-peak winter season, negotiate a discount if you're staying for several days, but bargaining is not the norm. Many upmarket hotels offer special weekend rates to fill rooms usually occupied by weekday business guests, so look into these mini-packages if you want to treat yourself to a weekend in a smart hotel. Most of the top hotels are centred around Knightsbridge, Mayfair and Belgravia. A double room in the famous Dorchester or Claridge's could cost £300+ per night, with a level of service commensurate with the price. International chains catering for business clients, such as the Hilton, Inter-Continental and Marriott are in a similar bracket.
Hostels: There'a a good choice of hostels, most charging £20 or so per person, including several members of the YHA; tel: (0870) 770 8868; www.yha.org.uk
Bed and Breakfasts are a relative bargain in price terms; ask the tourist office or use an agency. Some are **Welcome Homes**, tel: (0845) 370 9009; **London Homestead Services**, tel: (020) 7286 5115; and **LSE**, tel: (020) 7955 7575.
Self-catering apartments can offer good value for families, from about £250 a week (and up to ten times that!).

Eating Out

London restaurants cater to every taste and budget – the diversity is almost unmatched by any other capital city. Even traditional **British** cooking, once a by-word for stodgy food, has been revitalized by a new generation of chefs and can now hold its own against the classic cuisines. **French**, **Italian** and **Greek** restaurants are all very common, while virtually every other European cuisine, from Spanish to Swedish, is easy to find. Britain has long been known for its ethnic foods, particularly **Chinese** and **Indian**; **Turkish**, **Malaysian**, **Thai**, **Lebanese** and **Japanese** restaurants are numerous and most other national cuisines are represented.

In recent years **pub** food has improved enormously, and while it may be hard to find a freshly made sandwich in some areas, in others the range and quality of bar food is as good as some restaurants. There are also a number of **bistros** and **wine bars**, where as well as sampling a range of fine wines you can find salads, light meals, and other fare. If all else fails, a simple **café** or **tea-room** can provide snacks, sandwiches or a quick meal.

Transport

London Underground and London Buses operate a 24hr telephone service for travel information, tel: (020) 7222 1234. **Travel Information Centres** can provide useful free leaflets and pocket maps on bus and tube services; they are located at Piccadilly Circus tube station and at Euston, Victoria and Liverpool Street mainline stations, as well as in all four terminals at Heathrow Airport.

If you're planning to use public transport more than a couple of times a day, it's definitely worth getting a bus pass (covers bus travel only and is not valid 04:30–09:00) or an Oyster card, which covers buses, tubes and the DLR (Docklands Light Railway) – and also provides discounts on some river journeys. Both are available from most tube and mainline stations, as well as many newsagents. Travelcards (similar to Oyster) can be purchased only at mainline stations. Tube/DLR travel 04:30–09:30 is excluded from off-peak cards. Buses are cheaper than tubes, a fact reflected in the cost of bus passes.

Business Hours

Most **shops** are open at least 09:30–17:30, Mon–Sat, although different areas have their own late-night shopping days (Wed in Knightsbridge, Thu in Oxford Street, etc). Large supermarket chains stay open very late (some for 24 hours) Mon–Sat, and small corner shops (similar to convenience stores) stay open until 22:00 or later. Sunday trading is now firmly established in London, with supermarkets and many department stores open 12:00–16:00 or 18:00.

Office hours are usually 09:30–17:30, Mon–Fri (for **banks** see under **Money Matters**, p. 122). Office workers usually have a lunch hour between noon and 14:00. Opening hours of **Museums** and **tourist attractions** vary enormously, but most are open daily by 10:00 and close 17:30–18:30, with shorter hours on Sundays. Virtually everything stops on **Christmas Day** (including transport), but most establishments treat other public holidays (known as bank holidays) as Sundays.

CONVERSION CHART		
FROM	**TO**	**MULTIPLY BY**
Millimetres	Inches	0.0394
Metres	Yards	1.0936
Metres	Feet	3.281
Kilometres	Miles	0.6214
Square kilometres	Square miles	0.386
Hectares	Acres	2.471
Litres	Pints	1.760
Kilograms	Pounds	2.205
Tonnes	Tons	0.984
To convert Celsius to Fahrenheit: x 9 ÷ 5 + 32		

Time

During the winter Britain is on **Greenwich Mean Time** (GMT), and in summer (from March to October) on **British Summer Time** (BST) which is one hour ahead of GMT.
Europe: GMT plus 1hr.
USA, Canada (East): GMT minus 5hrs.
USA, Canada (West): GMT minus 8hrs.
Australia: GMT plus 8–10hrs.
New Zealand: GMT plus 12hrs.
South Africa: GMT plus 2hrs.

Communications

Post: Post offices are generally open 09:00–17:30, Mon–Fri; 09:00–12:30 or 13:00, Sat. The Trafalgar Square Post Office (24–28 William IV St) is open 08:00–20:00, Mon–Thurs; 08:30–20:00 Fri, 09:00–20:00 Sat. **Postage stamps** can be bought at post office counters, from vending machines, and in many newsagents.
Telephones: Public **payphones** are operated by British Telecom (BT) and most accept coins, credit cards and phonecards. **Phonecards** are available from post offices and newsagents and come in denominations of £3, £5, £10 and £20. A few payphones offer Internet access. London's area code is '020', followed by 8 digits. If you have old listings, use '020-7' in place of '0171' and '020-8' in place of '0181'. When calling within London, you need only the 8-digit number.

Numbers beginning '09' is premium rate (can be over £1 a minute) and numbers beginning '07' are mobiles (expensive). '0800' and '0808' are free lines. Try not to use the phone in your **hotel** room: mark-ups are among the world's highest. To make an international call, dial 00, followed by the country code and then the area code:
Australia 61
USA & Canada 1
Ireland 353
New Zealand 64
France 33
Singapore 65
Hong Kong 852
South Africa 27

GOOD READING

• Duncan, Andrew (1995) *Secret London*. New Holland, London. Explores little-known and hidden facets of the capital, with 20 miles of walks.
• Duncan, Andrew (1991) *Walking London*. New Holland, London. Features 30 original walks in and around the capital.
• Porter, Roy. *London: A Social History*. Hamish Hamilton. Engaging and comprehensive account of the capital's development.
• Tames, Richard (1992) *Traveller's History of London*. Windrush Press. A lively account of the capital's history, from Londinium to Docklands.
• Hamilton, Patrick. *20,000 Streets Under the Sky*. Hogarth/Trafalgar. Romantic trilogy set in the sleazy Soho of the 1930s.

Operator assistance 100
International Operator 155
Directory enquiries are no longer a BT (British Telecom) monopoly and are expensive. BT's numbers are: 118–500 for UK enquiries; 118–505 for overseas enquiries.

Electricity

The current is 240 volts AC (50 Hz). Most American or European appliances will need an adaptor – ask the hotel you're staying with if they can lend you one, otherwise try a chemist (pharmacist) or an electrical shop.

Weights and Measures

The imperial system of measurements has officially been replaced by the metric system, and that is used in shops, etc. (sometimes in tandem with imperial), but imperial is still common in speech.

Health Precautions

No special health precautions are necessary. Most European countries (and some in the Commonwealth) have reciprocal health arrangements should you need treatment at an NHS hospital; you will need to obtain the relevant forms before you leave home. For other nationalities, accident and emergency care is generally free at NHS hospitals' casualty departments, but there'll be a charge for other medical treatment (including hospitalization). It's therefore advisable to arrange comprehensive travel insurance before you leave home.

Personal Safety

Compared to many cities, London is a relatively safe destination and the greatest risk is from thieves and pickpockets hanging around busy shopping streets or on crowded underground platforms or trains. Use common sense.

• Don't carry more cash than you will need for the day.

• Keep your wallet or purse out of sight; keep handbags fastened and don't carry a wallet in your back pocket.

• Never leave a handbag, suitcase, or coat unattended.

• Avoid poorly lit, quiet areas (such as parks) after dark. If you are subject to a mugging or robbery, report it to the local police station (see under 'Police' in the phone book).

Emergencies

The familiar image of the British 'bobby' plodding the streets endures, although patrol cars now dominate. The police are generally approachable and helpful should you be lost or in trouble. In an emergency for police, fire, ambulance or coastguard dial 999 or 112.

Etiquette

London tends to be an easy-going place with very few formal dress codes or similar restrictions. A night at the opera or in a really top-class restaurant will, of course, necessitate more formal wear, but otherwise smart, casual clothes will do almost everywhere. The British are inveterate believers in **queueing**, whether it be at a bus stop, in shops or elsewhere, and don't

FESTIVALS AND EVENTS

Late Jan/early Feb • Chinese New Year
March • Ideal Home Exhibition, Chelsea Antiques Fair
Late March/early April •
Oxford v Cambridge Boat Race
April • Flora London Marathon
May • Chelsea Flower Show
Royal Windsor Horse Show
June • Trooping the Colour
Royal Academy Summer Exhibition (runs till Aug)
Derby Day and Royal Ascot
Biggin Hill Air Fair
Late June/early July • Henley Regatta
Wimbledon Lawn Tennis Championships
July • Farnborough Air Display
Kenwood Lakeside Concerts (run till Aug)
City of London Festival
Henry Wood Promenade Concerts (run till Sept)
August • Great British Beer Festival
Notting Hill Carnival
September • Chelsea Antiques Fair
Late Sept/early Oct • Horse of the Year Show
Costermongers Harvest Festival
November • Lord Mayor's Show
London to Brighton Veteran Car Rally
Guy Fawkes Night
State Opening of Parliament
Festival of Remembrance
December • International Showjumping

For a full rundown on special occasions get the monthly *London Planner*, a free and fairly comprehensive booklet from TICs (tourist information centres). To check the current events, consult the weekly listings magazines *Time Out* and *What's On* or the daily *Evening Standard*.

take kindly to those not prepared to stand in line for their turn. The exception is during the rush hour on tubes, buses and trains, when a free-for-all is more likely to prevail. On the Underground you stand on the right on escalators, and keep the left clear. In recent years **smoking** has become less acceptable in public places and is now totally banned on all **public transport** and in most public buildings. Restaurants and some hotels are now also increasingly anti-smoking: check before booking.

INDEX